PRAISES FOR THE SETUP

Finally, a read that is outside of the box. I've been long awaiting something that defies the traditional page turner and I think I've found it.

-Janet Jenkins-

Entertaining and full of character. The Setup allows you to let your imagination soar.

-Ed Rosin-

An enjoyable read. I loved the poetry intertwined throughout the book. It made for a very interesting read.

-Jessica Reed-

SHERIKA
FRAZIER
DUNCAN

THE
SETUP

WWW.13THANDJOAN.COM

The Setup

Copyright © 2019 by Sherika Frazier Duncan

All rights reserved. No part of this publication may be reproduced, distributed, or transmitted in any form or by any means, including photocopying, recording, or other electronic or mechanical methods, without the prior written permission of the publisher, except in the case of brief quotations embodied in critical reviews and certain other noncommercial uses permitted by copyright law. For permission requests, write to the publisher, addressed "Attention: Permissions Coordinator," 500 N. Michigan Avenue, Suite #600, Chicago, IL 60611.

13th & Joan books may be purchased for educational, business or sales promotional use. For information, please email the Sales Department at sales@13thandjoan.com.

First Edition Printed, January 2019

Library of Congress Cataloging-in-Publication Data has been applied for.

ISBN: 978-1-7335154-3-6

Printed in USA by 48HrBooks (www.48HrBooks.com)

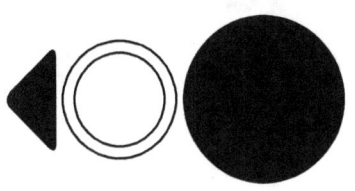

DEDICATION

For Nia Janae & Nyles J'Sean Duncan

Taufiqamri, Graphic Designer
Model: Nia Janae
www.theofficialniajanae.com

Little Nia

Lord help me.
Help me to be patient.
Lord help me to learn how
to be understanding and caring.
When she's blue, Lord provide me
with encouraging words.
Help me to nurture my innocent young offspring.
Mommy's mini-me is so intelligent
and so carefree.
Help me be of wisdom
to learn and to understand.
Please help me, Lord Jesus,
to cope with her becoming a young woman.
Give me the words to achieve.
Give me the words to explain life's cycle
of the birds and the bees.
Bless the person who
takes care of her while
Mommy and Daddy go off to work.
Help them be patient and calm
whenever her little voice chirps.

Nyles River

*My spring of everlasting love flows
continuously for you.
As long as the Sahara Desert
and as sweet as Louisiana's sugar cane iced tea.
You have completed Mommy's legacy.*

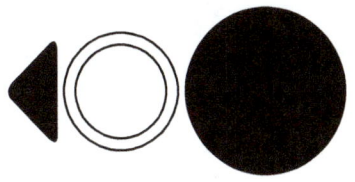

EPIGRAPH

"The story picked up the pen and began to tell the ink all about how things happened. The ink began writing it all down."

~Rika Epiphanies

www.rikaepiphanies.com

Taufiqanvi, Graphic Designer

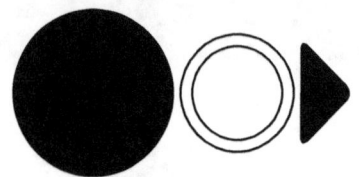

DEAR READER,

Nothing about this story is traditional in the way that it is told. Tradition has a way of holding us back from our truths. My intent was to capture the elements and feelings of the characters portrayed, while allowing a series of events to unfold. This book has been written to make your imagination soar.

An uncut version of events that have taken place is extraordinarily incomparable to any other book of fiction. The content presented is meant to spark a series of emotional reactions. These experiences are ones that we encounter throughout the span of a lifetime, inclusive of happiness, sadness, disappointment, and fear. The idea is to reflect and visualize. In what direction do you see yourself heading? Will you accept the calling to live out your deepest dreams and aspirations?

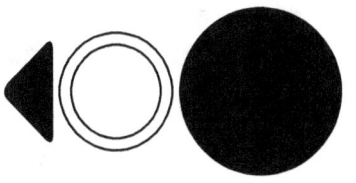

PREFACE:
DIVINE INTERVENTION

The purpose of this book is to provide a point of reference for life and reflection amidst points in time where things don't always go according to plan. This book depicts a more realistic approach to how we deal with trials and tribulations that often distract us from our happiness. My hope is that this book will help tackle significant issues such as: relationships, self-confidence, and peer pressure regarding sex, drugs, alcohol, and death. This book is filled with survival tips, inspiration, courage, determination, and self-identity.

Written specifically for people who have a willingness to discover their best lives, even when faced with setbacks, the viewpoints outlined are for people who have been disappointed and brokenhearted and unaware of how they will overcome it all. This is for the college graduate who is embarking upon adulthood, or the high school freshman experiencing social change. This content and message is geared towards African-American family members who have secrets and those who have never received the proper treatment to truly heal from their internal pain. Lastly, this is for anyone desiring to learn how to overcome oppression. From homelessness, to human-trafficking, workplace bullying issues, and everything in between, there is a sign of hope within these pages for anyone who reads. This book is for anyone who has ever experienced feelings of doubtfulness to succeed or the feeling of failure. We must learn to discover our self-identity.

After learning who we are as a people, we can come to recognize the multitude of roles we play and the process of finding peace internally. We have experienced uncomfortable circumstances, and even trauma, that must be overcome. Childhood traumatic events or abuse can affect us in different ways. Childhood trauma can impact us as adults by forcing us to revisit painful pasts. Fresh wounds can linger into adulthood due to neglect and buried emotions. We become victimized by believing that there are no other alternatives to what has happened to us, and we often feel imprisoned from the painful memories that continue to haunt us based on unknown triggers. The need to suppress the anger inside grows until it becomes second nature. In these instances, we have the potential to cause pain, not only to ourselves, but to others. The whole cycle of the unknown parts of ourselves is a new normal, and acceptable. Because there is no desire to want to discover our best life in determining who we want to be in this world, the aforementioned can have a significant impact on our psyche, our health, relationships, and our survival.

All of the aforementioned obstacles unfolds through the eyes of the fictional characters featured in this book. They all represent some imperfection or challenge; and the way they chose to deal with the outcomes determines the type of quality of life they possess. This book seeks to reveal how to interpret or adhere to the many setups or situations that place us on a different course in life, whether temporarily or permanently. These setups are deliberately conditioned to allow us to believe in a limited and controlled manner. The life we live has been passed down in communication using high profile tragedies, news media outlets, radio, television, politics, education, sports, music, drugs, crime relations, religion, science, and government of what defines normalcy. It is very confusing to interpret and decipher what normalcy is through all the speculated information.

Today, we must learn to verify the sources of information that we allow to serve as indicators for who we are and what we believe about ourselves. These observations cause stress, and the majority are not willing to put the extra time to research and challenge the status quo due to laziness, limited time, or lack of know-how. So, it is highly acceptable to rely on entertainment such as the world wide web, popular social media outlets, YouTube bloggers, speculated rumors and news to tell the story. It will take a tragedy to shift the way we are currently accustomed to feeling and thinking...Since we believe we have it made due to everything already done for us. It plays a pivotal role in delaying our pursuit of happiness to the fullest. We can perform our research and make our observations to determine the best results for our own lives. Public announcement of fear tactics or government agenda should not stir us into acceptance mode. The signs of war, violence, legal frustrations and the most trick of the trade money cannot be the deciding factors for all our decision making. Even though, in this society, those practices set the standards. Fear cannot be the solution to our destination or reality; no longer should it make or persuade us into a plateau. Respect, love, and freedom can restore the purpose of our existence. History must be redefined and scrutinized. Our food system needs re-evaluating, and our medical standards need additional revisions. The scholar or scientist and physician are all a part of the same governing entities consistently explaining how things are perceived to be. Workplace bullying, human trafficking, drug, and alcohol abuse, are at an all-time high. The Friday during Super Bowl 2019, did you notice that police cracked down and made forty arrests for sex-trafficking in metro Atlanta? Our mental health is at stake of being affected by what we put inside our bodies. Healing is the key to discovering our real freedom of tapping into our fullest potential as human beings. This novel is a gift to remind us all the importance of re-defining who we are as a people, while discovering our ancestry spiritual belief in strengthening as one to address the things mentioned in this material and more.

Deeply Rooted

Keep me deeply rooted in the dreams and broken promises
Let every sound echo across the Great Wall of China,
with the sweet aroma of herbal cranberry tea cleansing
and comparable to a heartfelt melody;
So, when I tremble to fall,
Place me firmly on Mount Everest, standing resiliently tall
Keep me deeply rooted to our children's needs
As I encourage them to express their intellect and freedom of speech;
Provide them with wisdom on expressing their artistic ability
sketched across a mass canvas
Circumferences all understanding,
transcribing objects into words
As we dance to the African beats in unison
Reserving a moment to sweep away
human litter alongside our streets.
Giving thanks to the Creator for all things and for paving the way
As we embrace opportunities to showcase
our hidden, untapped talents.

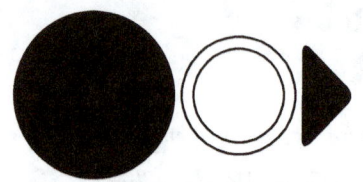

ACKNOWLEDGEMENTS

(My Parents Pictured: Mr. & Mrs. Walter Frazier, Sr.)

    I want to acknowledge and celebrate my creator, our heavenly father of life and the source of all. To my loving, supportive family for their guidance, and contributions, and for being patient and understanding during this project. I humbly honor and pay tribute by uplifting the resilient ancestral lineage that paved the way before me and watches over my family. I thank you (Lola Ausgood, George Cherry, Christopher & Patsy Barfield, Joseph & Rosa

Major Barfield) for all of the necessary intercessions made on our family behalf regarding health, money, protection, career and any past current and future mortal affairs. Specifically the ones of my loving paternal mother, Clara Barfield Frazier's bloodline: Barfield-Major; and paternal father, Henry Frazier's bloodline: Frazier. In addition, to the ones of my sweet maternal mother, Rosa Mae Cherry's bloodline: Cherry-Ausgood; and maternal father Ulysses "Buddy" Grant Balloon's families. May we continue to show love to one another, is my sincere prayer. Also, acknowledging my conceptual child, Excellence Dance Studio, Inc., may you forever live on to do miraculous things in the years to come. My dearest friends, Tiffany Cason Hamilton, Tamara Moore Ross, Tammatha Grice Proby, Tillie Hogans, VaLisa Miller McGhee, Jackie Johnson, Vickie Gordon, Tanya Gallon, Rolande Mehu, Chantae Spann, and Derek Bell. Lastly, I am very grateful to my multi-talented publishing company, 13th and Joan, for their devoted mentorship and excellent delivery and professionalism which exceeded my expectations. Kudos to my dedicated mentor and fellow FAMU alumnus friend, Ardre Orie, and her outstanding team.

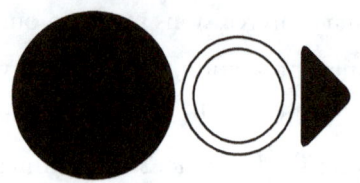

CHARACTER SKETCHES

Penelope Lee

"Yes darling, of course I will add money to your commissary."
Meet Penelope, aka Penny

Penelope Lee is a business professional, and a former HBCU homecoming queen while attending San Diego College in her hometown of San Diego, California. She relocated to Atlanta after getting married to her longtime boyfriend, Jeff, aka Gunna. Hard times happened for both of them when Jeff was sentenced to serve time for his involvement in a *get rich quick scheme* gone wrong, and she landed a high paying contract assignment for a group of workplace bullies.

PENELOPE LEE, better known as, Penny, is one of the main characters who has ties to the group of women associated in this novel. She relocated from San Diego, California to Madison, Georgia in her early youth to stay with her Aunt Betsey. She is a dear friend, problem solver and comforter. She is a great sounding board and provides unbiased input to life's situations and often takes on the role of a relationship expert. Her husband, Jeff, is incarcerated in the Augusta Correctional Center in the state of Virginia, for child support, which led to a DUI, violation of probation, and a get rich scheme gone wrong. To deal with the stress of being a loving, devoted wife, confidante, and stepmother to five children, Penny consumes herself with staying busy in her spare time. She is currently working in a highly stressful environment and experiencing workplace bullying. She was strategically set up to be demoted based on dislike from two women of her own race, RASPUTIA and LUCINDA. Little did Penny know, they despised her decision to keep things professional in the workplace. She did not desire to engage in social activities with those groups of women.

Tremaine Lewis

"Hey honey, guess what?"

Meet Tremaine, aka Tre

Tremaine Lewis is a single black islander, known as a wild firecracker from Castle Hill, Bronx, New York. She moved to Atlanta to pursue her dreams in the cosmetology industry in 2000. She possesses a strong sense of awareness in this man-made world.

TREMAINE LEWIS occasionally referred to as, Tre, is an Afro-Caribbean, wild, firecracker from Castle Hill, New York. Tremaine experienced a tough upbringing without having a father figure involved to protect her. She was introduced to the street life very fast. She is well-equipped to educate the community about the injustices in society regarding social change, the food system, law enforcement, racial profiling, and dreamer movement in a socially conscious era.

Chloe Steele

"Oh really, what's the name of this sleeping medicine?"

Meet Chloe aka, Introvert

Chloe Steele is a highly intuitive individual who is continually thinking. She is originally from Madison County, Georgia, "Home of the Mighty Bulldog."

CHLOE STEELE has been a very reserved, cognitive thinker her entire life, due to her extreme anxiety. The frequent nightmares she has experienced since childhood still taunt her. These patterns are a few of the reasons why she is seeking professional help to eliminate the possibility of depression, panic disorders, and her short attention span.

Giani LoveHart

"I haven't seen her just yet. I plan to encourage her to not give up, girl."

Meet Giani, aka Gigi

Gigi LoveHart is a smart, freelance artist, social butterfly, nurturing, extrovert; and graduate of Elizabeth City State University in Elizabeth City, North Carolina. She moved to Atlanta to reunite with her family and friends.

GIGI LOVEHART is full of life, talkative, and an assertive, positive spirit. The self-employed, freelance artist thoroughly enjoys her independent lifestyle. She is the voice of reason in most cases for friends and family.

Simone Bison

"I am trying to understand how I managed to allow this depression to manifest in my life?"

Meet Simone, aka Cece

Simone Bison is a loving, devoted housewife, and aspiring fashion designer who drives for Uber as a hobby in Atlanta, Georgia. She and her husband Charles are expecting their first child soon.

SIMONE BISON routinely predicts her day to be filled with nausea and bloatedness from her second pregnancy, intertwined with household chores, daily errands for her family business affairs, along with caring for her husband, Charles,' personal needs.

Anastasia Olay

"Oh Lord, now you tell me? Don't you think I would've appreciated this information prior to this moment?"

Meet Anastasia Olay, aka Lady Anaconda

Dr. Anastasia Olay is a charming, down to earth, influential psychologist who is very well-versed in many fields, including personality, behavioral, and social cognitive psychology. Globally, she conducts groundbreaking studies and innovative research throughout the country.

ANASTASIA OLAY is a licensed psychologist and acclaimed keynote speaker who makes life changing breakthroughs around the country. Her contributions were pivotal in the discovery of freedom for embracing internal healing abroad.

Charles Bison

"Are you joining the #MeToo movement now? All I am saying is that Uber ain't cutting it to maintain everything we got going on, let alone another mouth to feed."

Meet Charles, aka Chuck

Chuck is a graduate of Florida Agricultural & Mechanical University's School of Business & Industry. He also earned his Master's degree in Business Administration. Six years ago, he started his own company, Bison MediaCom. The business made the annual list of the top Fortune 500 companies according to Fortune Magazine. He is Simone's husband and the two have been together for six years.

Jeffrey Lee

"Baby, I need to get tuna, chili, drinks and Little Debbie snacks."

Meet Jeffrey, aka Jeff

He is a resourceful, hardworking father of five children from his previous relationships before marrying Penelope. Jeff is incarcerated in the Augusta Correctional Center in the state of Virginia, for child support, which led to DUI, violation of probation and a get rich quick scheme gone wrong. He is currently serving time in prison for his unlawful involvement.

Travis Garnett

"The very first moment I saw you, I envisioned you by my side as my queen."

Meet Travis

Travis is a certified fitness trainer and seasoned spinning instructor. He spends most of his time assisting others with discovering a healthier version of themselves, while pursuing his dreams of opening up his very own 24 hour fitness gym.

Katina Rozell

"Discuss? Discuss what? Look lady, I don't know anything. I'm just out here surviving."

Meet Katina

Katina was in a safe house after her family disowned her at an early age. She became involved in a dysfunctional, toxic relationship with her boyfriend, who introduced her to drugs. The use of opioids aided in her manipulation that led to her involvement in sex trafficking.

TABLE OF CONTENTS

Dedication v
    Little Nia vii
    Nyles River viii
Epigraph ix
Dear Reader x
Preface: Divine Intervention xi
    Deeply Rooted xv
Acknowledgements xvi
Character Sketches xviii

Chloe 1
Tremaine 4
    My Nubian Sister, Hold On! 9
    Epiphany: Culturally Free! 10
Tremaine 12
    Mysterious Friend 14
Penelope 15
    A Breath Of Fresh Air 16
Penelope 17
    Epiphany: Lovely Elevated Steps! 19
    Epiphany: An Embodiment Of Doubt 20
Tremaine 22
    At Last 24
    Epiphany: Particles Of Your Worth 25

Simone 26
    Epiphany: Complacent Love 28
        Busy Bee 29
Penelope 30
        Laundry 34
Gigi 36
    Epiphany: Uninvited Stupidity! 38
Gigi 40
    Epiphany: The Philosophy Of Elevated Chatter 41
Gigi 42
    Epiphany: Donors Of Repetitive Character Assassination
    45
Gigi 47
    Epiphany: Anybody Have A Heart? 48
Chloe 49
    Epiphany: An Ocean Of Dreams! 50
Chloe 52
        The Intellectual Virus 54
        Cyber Love 56
Dr. Anastasia Olay 57
        Southern Girl 59
    Epiphany: Consciously Speaking In A Lifetime! 61
Dr. Anastasia Olay 63
Introduction To Rika's Epiphanies 67
    Epiphany: Evidence Of Acid Tears! 68
        Precisely Yours 69
Tremaine 70

Temptation 71
Tremaine 73
    Epiphany: Tainted Dreams 75
Tremaine 77
    Epiphany: Longing For Sandcastles 81
        Fantasy 82
Chloe 83
    Epiphany: Iced Pumped Hearts! 87
Dr. Anastasia Olay 88
        Unforgettable 92
    Epiphany: Consciously Intoxicating 94
Simone 95
    Epiphany: Levels To This! 97
Simone 98
        Black Gyrl 100
Gigi 101
    Epiphany: Predisposed Booby Traps 103
Gigi 104
        Hearts 105
Gigi 106
    You Are Black As 107
Tremaine 108
    Epiphany: Granted Gratitude 110
Tremaine 112
        Trapped 114
    Epiphany: Illogical Behavior 116
Penelope 118

- 3d Glasses ... 120
- Epiphany: Flawless Errors! ... 122
- Penelope ... 123
  - Envy Don't Hate Me ... 125
  - Epiphany: Scorched Opponents ... 127
- Penelope ... 128
  - Burglar ... 131
  - Epiphany: Ravenous Visions! ... 132
- Dr. Anastasia Olay ... 133
  - Seconds To Minute ... 134
- Dr. Anastasia Olay ... 136
  - Epiphany: A Multitude Of Refractions In Multiple Distractions ... 142
- Dr. Anastasia Olay ... 144
  - Please Don't Take My Sunshine Away ... 148
  - Epiphany: Enchanted Noises! ... 149
- Chloe ... 151
  - If You Wanna Know How I Feel ... 152
- Chloe ... 154
  - You Make Me Melt ... 156
- Simone ... 158
  - Speechless ... 159
- Simone ... 160
  - Epiphany: Traumatic Truths ... 162
- Gigi ... 163
- Tremaine ... 168
  - Epiphany: Selfish Traces Of Tacky Footprints ... 170

Chloe 172
    Epiphany: Artistic Influence! 173
Tremaine 174
    Epiphany: Orchestrated Steps! 176
Simone 178
    Epiphany: Your Outlook On Life 181
Resources 183
About The Author 185
Connect With Sherika Duncan 187

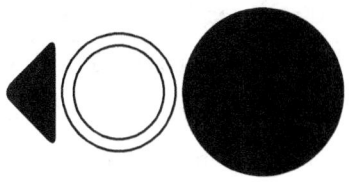

CHLOE

"After several sounds ricocheted through the thin wall, the D.J. stopped spinning the music and the lights came on. There he was, in a pool of blood, lying face down right next to me. Suddenly, another round of bullets fired as I looked up to get a glimpse of Malcolm's killer. After the killer shot Malcolm in cold blood, he then pointed the gun in the air, blasting off more rounds."

Dr. Olay interrupted. "Chloe, at such a young age, it must have been a traumatizing experience to be held captive without any way out."

Chloe laid there in her psychologist's office in the striped lounge, cushy couch clinching on to one of the accent pillows tightly to her chest. It was like she was on an amusement ride trying to hold on to keep from falling. In the background, there was a timer beeping, and suddenly, she opened her eyes. Glancing over at the nearby bookcase, the clock stood there sounding the alarm, facing Dr. Anastasia Olay.

"I believe our session is over, Chloe. We are making great progress. I hope to see you in a week."

The doctor's office building was located right in the heart of downtown Atlanta. The environment seemed to promote recovery, restoration, independence and a better quality of life. The tall, majestic, cathedral-like structure possessed bulky piers and rounded Greek arches with well-defined columns attached in the existing construction. It was truly a vision to see; one of many highlights of the busy city. Chloe always felt cozy and inspired visiting this particularly-premeditated space. Yet, the invasion of taunted memories from three-decade-old tragedy replayed through her mind nonstop. Dr. Olay swore that Chloe could be healed of her panic attacks and severe migraine headaches once she tackled the underlying root cause. Although, deep down inside, she feels there can be another alternative than remembering that tragic night.

As she was leaving out of the gothic two-story building, she noticed the zigzag patterns, repeating half-circle columns trimmed in carved stones approaching the nearby Marta train station farther along on Northwest Peachtree Street. The temperature was pleasantly cool, considering the season.

While in the station corridor, Chloe's phone rang. When the Marta stopped, she walked up and tapped her Breeze card on the target to open the fare gates, and answered her phone. "I know. I know, Tre. I am late."

The voice on the other end spoke, "Chloe, you're always late!"

She was already prepared to clap back. "I am en route and close by."

Tre's unconvinced, high-pitched voice burst out "Ok, well you need to be here in the next thirty minutes, or else Penny and I will expect a large shot of double espressos with ginseng after spin class...all sponsored by you. Got it?"

Chloe was completely convinced that Tremaine was a straight hustler as she replied, "Yeah yeah, see you in a sec."

Chloe was almost certain that Tremaine hung up the phone and said to Penelope, "Girl, she is probably taking the scenic route. So, we'll probably get our double espressos." And, she could bet that Penelope giggled and said, "Girl, you are crazy."

Chloe arrived shortly after, and Tremaine and Penelope were both snickering as she came into the door. Tremaine began to speak first. "Well, I need to mentally and physically prepare for this experience," she said. "So, I'll just start stretching to warm-up these old fragile bones of mine."

Chloe agreed by pointing her finger around in a fast-circular motion while shaking her head in agreement. She was invisibly marking off their proximity where she assumed they would most likely congregate. "Yes, girl," she said. "Because, we don't need your bones talking and disturbing our concentration while spinning up and through here."

In Vain

Nothing is impossible when you are hopeful, because what we tell ourselves determines how we live, feel, and operate in this world. Show support for people you empower by making them aware that you believe in them wholeheartedly without anything in return. Giving to others without expectation of receiving anything in return will make someone feel more connected to you and appreciated by you.

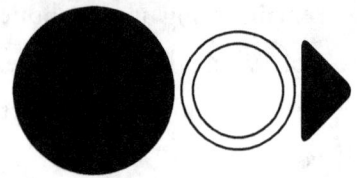

TREMAINE

Chloe walked into the spinning room and greeted Tremaine and Penelope. "Hey ladies, sorry I am late. My last meeting of the day ran a bit over," she announced.

Penelope replied, as she started to begin her stretching, "Hey girl, you're just in time. We were just about to do these stretches."

While Chloe was stretching, she stared at her brittle legs in disbelief. Her legs were very similar to a type of spider Tremaine remembered seeing as a child. She called it a "Daddy Long Legs Spider." The position of her elongated, slender legs appeared juxtaposed as if they were made from Play-Doh, due to her awkward stretching technique. Tremaine attempted to refrain from laughing aloud. She stood there a minute and had her very own Chloe roasting party while tickled with laughter inside. As she was trying to pull herself together, she said "Wait, please don't tell me. Chloe, you are going back up there to that Psych Lady Anaconda!?"

Chloe clapped back then rolled her head with attitude. "Her name is, Dr. Anastasia Olay," she replied.

Tremaine picked up a bottle of 9.5+ pH balanced alkaline spring water with electrolytes, and removed the cap, while doing a side eye before taking a sip. She glanced at her, and acknowledged the correction. "Yeah, that's what I said." She nodded her head to signal that she was not interested. "Anyhow, all you need to do is get laid and inhale, while smudging some quality sage."

"Smudging sage?" Penelope asked, in disbelief.

"Hell yeah! Baby, don't sleep on sage. It will get rid of all that emotional crap going on with you, all while balancing your chakra. The smudging will concentrate on purging the negative energy while restoring your mind."

Chloe cosigned then said, "This is getting very enlightening. I always wanted to try smudging. So, how do you go about smudging, again?"

"First, you will need to get you one of those herb wands..."

Penelope interrupted, "Herb wands? What the hell? Remember, the last time Tre gave advice, she was helping her mother make salmon croquettes in a cast iron skillet. She was fifteen then, and the pan exploded on the stovetop into pieces." They all laughed in amusement.

"I know these tricks, hear me? And, that happened roughly two decades ago. It's safe to trust me! Anyhow, your mind must be prepared and focused, then you light the wand to start blowing out the flame. I'm trying to put you on to game. The herbs will smolder and smoke to prevent it from burning. You use a candle instead of a match or a regular type of lighter."

Chloe lifted only one of two of her recently threaded thick arched eyebrows. She slowly started to lose interest. "Tremaine, that's too much," she said. "Who is going to remember all of this? You just said go here, jump three times, then a white unicorn will appear. Afterwards, the unicorn will turn into a vampire. You must allow the vampire to bite you on the neck right before the werewolves devour you. Then, to keep from being eaten, you must wave the wand around to prevent the wicked witch from burning you up. Come on!"

Penelope added, "Ha! In other words, where's the manual?"

Tremaine replied in defense, "Alright, I see you got jokes, Coachella. Uh hmm, well there will be a time in your life where you will need to cleanse a space by slowly walking around the room, or multiple rooms, while focusing on clearing out negative energy. When that's not enough, Ba-by, I don't know, you might just need to invest in a good white or rose quartz pendant to wear on you frequently."

Penelope side-eyed Tremaine like she didn't have anything important to say. "Girl, how did your session go? Did she crack the code this time?" she asked Chloe.

"No. She thinks the trauma that I'm facing may have plenty to do with the lack of affection shown as a child, now," Chloe replied, before turning her attention back to Tremaine. "Tremaine, say no to drugs, okay?" She continued to ramble. "Well, all I know is the American Psychological Association should pay me for all the countless hours I am laying in the chair in disbelief."

Tremaine was panting from being out of breath from reaching her final plank exercise set. Penelope was kneeled securely while tying her fluorescent yellow shoestrings. "I must say, though, my emotional state has improved over the years, compared to all of us. We deal with things differently. So, back off my Chaka Khan, why don't ya?" Chloe demanded.

"See, I choose not to put up with this foolishness. As the late Queen of Soul, Aretha Franklin, would say, R.E.S.P.E.C.T!"

Then, Tremaine shouted, "CHAK-RA!" Chloe began to swing her head up and down while murmuring, "Yeah, that exactly."

As we were all standing up inside our invisible, designated area Tremaine previously formed, a very tall Caucasian gym member invaded and said, "Excuse me, you are blocking access to the water fountain area. Can you move somewhere out of the path?"

Tremaine freely answered, "Dear, White People."

"Tremaine!" yelled Chloe and Penelope.

The Caucasian gym member replied, "What did you just say to me, nigger?"

"Baby! You Lord of the Rings, Smeagol look alike; you don't want none of this." Tremaine began to bobble her head from side to side while rubbing her hands together like she was about to get ready to tear into some hot fried catfish at Big Momma's house.

Chloe cowardly responded, "Tremaine, shut your black self-up! You're going to get us kicked out of here!"

Tremaine just couldn't believe it. "Why are you coming for me? You are really reminding me of some type of token black person right now."

"Are you being serious right now? Tremaine, what are you talking about?" Chloe asked.

"Seriously, I don't believe they are going there. No one is checking her? You are so conditioned towards thinking that its abnormal to stand up for ourselves as a people. I hope you know that black lives still matter!"

Penelope interjected, "Tre, you think you are better than everybody!"

Tremaine answered, "No, I'm just trying to do my best. There is a difference between desiring to be the best and flaunting it. Newsflash, we not trying to make the word *nigger* great again. So, you are sounding very much like the Minnesota House candidate dude who's running for state representative using the same negative word right now, Chloe."

Penelope understood she was expected to choose a side. "I think Chloe is just saying, chill out, Tremaine."

"Chloe has some serious nerve to be upset with me for defending the black movement in America. We are quick to use the N-word as a trend amongst each other. We use the word in our music, and even in our movies. Then, we are quick to go ham when they use it," Tremaine replied, nodding her head continuously.

My Nubian Sister, Hold On!

My Nubian sister, hold on
to a strength that is deep in you;
When times are troubled, and things look blue;
sister, strive for motivation;
A force or will to succeed...
Don't worry yourself, sister.
Call on the Man who holds the key.
The ridicule and the temperament will all come to an end,
once you look within yourself and find your true friend.
Self-esteem is her name. She'll support your every word,
you'll never feel ashamed.
My Nubian sister you will see the change,
then you will know what the future will bring...
So, this is where you belong,
my Nubian black princess,
HOLD ON!

Epiphany: Culturally Free!

During the Celebration of Independence, we are reminded of our freedom. It is a constant reflection of our individual freedoms in our society. We must take active initiative to research our own history. We are accustomed to being in a classroom setting and allowing an expert to explain who we are.

We must research how we came into America and our family tree. It is when we make profound noise, address educational bullying, and racial challenges in our society that we can begin to understand our roots. It is so necessary to have a sound opinion about these matters. We all have different patterns of thought. These thinking tanks represent the beauty of ideas. Can you imagine if George Washington Carver didn't create multiple inventions from a small source of protein called the peanut?

There is an invention inside of us that we have yet to speak or write down. There are several people that are mutely insecure because of others who they feel may be more educated. Some see their credentials as a form of bullying others who don't possess any accolades.

It is very acceptable for the educated individual's thoughts or opinions to have more value. Racial challenges exist throughout our society, even in the highest house of the land, the White House. When we voted our 44th President, Barack Hussein Obama II into office, it was based on the people's choice. It was not acceptable for some people due to a strong racial climate.

Our employment, school systems, and daily interactions still demonstrate that racial challenges exist. On Independence Day, we should account for the ability to be culturally free. We have the power to change the atmosphere. We must possess self-confidence and the ability to communicate effectively towards seeking our own history.

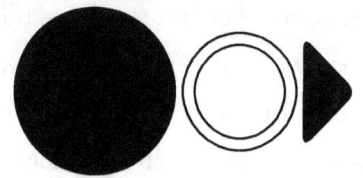

TREMAINE

The slight commotion seemed to have caught the attention of the spinning instructor.

"Excuse me ladies, is everything alright?" he asked.

Tremaine immediately answered, "Finally. Because, we need some straightening. See, somebody needs to come check Miss Becky."

Chloe interrupted, "Yes, we're fine. Our friend is just extremely exhausted from tonight's workout. Great work."

"Thank you. Well, I'm Travis. Whenever you think of anyone needing private, in- person, or online customized sessions, be sure to let me know. I have openings for new clients, as well. Here's my card. Contact me."

Tremaine gathered up her towel, water bottle, and bag, then pulled out her wireless Beats by Dre. She powered on her Bluetooth to connect the phone to her headset. Now, Tremaine was seriously multi-tasking, as, she observed Chloe innocently marking her territory. Tremaine was peeping game, while secretly made a call using her headset.

Meanwhile, Chloe continued to entertain, Travis. "Pleased to meet you, Travis. I am Chloe. These are my friends, Tremaine and Penelope."

Tremaine waved a hello while leaving a voicemail message. "Hey, I am on the way now to our spot, Baby. Bye" She hung up the phone and walked off then gathered her belongings.

"Well, I have been seriously thinking about adding a different fitness and diet routine to my schedule," Chloe told Travis.

Travis nodded, "Yeah? Well, there you go. Hit me up. I'd love to work it out with you. I meant work out with you, of course."

Penelope shrugged as she said to Chloe, "Now there's a whole lot of tea being served tonight. You got Tre setting up a booty call and you setting up one on one wrestling sessions."

Chloe shook her head in disbelief, then said, "Girl, it's just a freaking online workout program."

Penelope slanted her eyes at Chloe, and murmured, "Uh huh."

"I don't know what you are talking about. I'm just trying to go and get my sleeping medicine as usual," Tremaine said to Penelope.

Chloe chimed in while laughing, "Oh, really? What's the name of this sleeping medicine?"

Tremaine threw her hands up and surrendered then walked away. "Look, I'll see you chicks later. Deuces."

Mysterious Friend

*Mysterious friend with no name,
what shall I call you?
You're different from the same.
When gray clouds of thunder roll in,
you were there for me when the rain came.
And although neither one of us wants to admit,
it was as if a tornado touched down and hit
us both in the heart,
with the arrow of Cupid's dart.
Overly protective as a mother with a newborn child, giving another
a chance
to move in churns your heart inside and out.
So, what shall I call you?
I need to know.
Lover? Friend? Foe?
Because boyfriend may be inappropriate, it may corrupt
your image. So, what shall I call you?
I'm running out of minutes Bennett!*

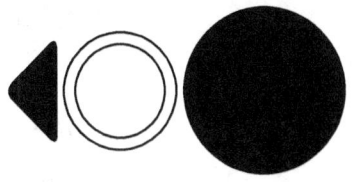

PENELOPE

As Tremaine dashed out in a hurry, Penelope stood there in the doorway of the gym with Chloe. They watched Tremaine leave out like a bat out of hell. Penelope recapped, "Yeah some sleeping medicine, right?"

Chloe said, "You know, I'm beginning to think that starting my fitness plans may be perfect timing after all. It could be the key to solving these anxiety attacks."

Penelope agreed. "That sounds like a plan, Chloe. I hope so. Let me know how it goes. Listen, I'll see ya later, Sis." Penelope walked away signaling arm movement towards a car with a pink hue sign on the dashboard. She looked back at Chloe and said, "There's my Lyft."

"Ok, Penny, see you later."

The drive seemed like forever and the walk from the lobby to Penelope's apartment was even longer. She finally put the keys in the door to reach peace and quiet inside.

A Breath of Fresh Air

*A breath of fresh air is essential
to the heart to operate.
To have potential,
to face this dreadful place,
filled with polluted air,
infectious disease,
deadly germs lingering in the trees.
The cough of one next to you
and the constant smell of smoke
which turns your face blue.
The dreadful smell of an unclean person
and the filthy mouth of somebody cursing
dampers the vision of a yellow rose in the midst of the deep forest.
Or the constant harassment of bill collectors
calling to say that, "you owe us."
But, while you were there
in the heat of it all
just reflecting on that delicate
flower bursting, vaporizing clean, moist
a breath of fresh air
to hold you over as you return to this cruel world of deep concern.*

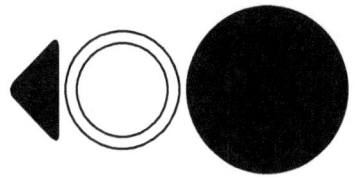

PENELOPE

Penelope could almost hear the bathtub calling her name. *"Penelope,"* it faintly said. She was almost delusional from being so tired, while placing the keys on the granite countertop. "Alexa, play smooth jazz," Penelope requested, as she gladly stripped naked to enter the shower. She changed the dial to a nice, steamy and warm temperature. Penelope wasn't in it fifteen minutes when her phone began ringing. It was like the caller had eyes on her at that very moment saying, *"Pick up. I know you see me calling you like a bill collector."* Whoever it may have been was really asking for a mouth full.

"Hello!" Penelope put the call on speaker, as she stood in her master bathroom mirror looking soaked and wet, drying off in preparation of getting dressed. "Simone...oh, gurl...see...you were about to...oh. Hold up, hold up...slow down...what? You aren't worried about Chuck, again? Look, it's not doing you or the baby any good to be worried about his whereabouts!"

Simone replied, "I'm working a couple of hours tonight."

Penelope put her head down and placed one hand on her forehead. "Ubering at 11:30 PM? You need to be home with your feet propped up and resting and feeding that fetus growing inside of you. I am sure Charles has a logical explanation for not coming home from work just yet."

Simone raised her voice with uncertainty, "I don't know, maybe he does."

Penelope looked into the mirror to see her body was still damp. "Please go home and call me when you are there in the house! Where's the trust in your husband? Married people, we are a trip! I mean, why get married when you ain't comfortable with your partner's decisions? Please understand that I am not picking on you. I pose this question routinely to my married and engaged friends and co-workers. It must be a trend or something. Almost like you all texting each other, 'well mine just left' and 'mine not home yet,' or 'mine just said he or she was going to the gym." Get out of here!"

Simone defensively said,"That's not funny, Penny."

Penelope put the call on speaker to finish drying off, then proceeded to get dressed. "Seriously, it really makes the single life lifestyle appealing to me. I can do bad by my damn self, with plenty of rest, too. Oh, ok well after this Uber customer transaction is done, please let that be your very last business for tonight. GET HOME, SIMONE! Bye, chile."

Epiphany: Lovely Elevated Steps!

Picture this...an era in our whole society so full of life. I see images of our people actively staying true to themselves and remaining loyal to their inner strengths. These visions are electrifying where we are stepping up to the plate and refraining from being emotionally attached to our outcomes.

There exists an inner voice inside of us, pinching our brains, persuading us to be more. Yes, it takes an extra burst of confidence to elevate our creativity. We can imagine a place where our seeds can nourish and multiply into greatness. Maslow's hierarchy of needs states, our motivations stem from self-actualization, esteem, safety, physiological, and most importantly, love.

As we perform routine inventories of our gifts, there is a need to know who we are to define where we are going in the future. It builds upon our chase to constantly race to achieve the next accomplishment. These experiences will gain self-respect and respect from others. There is a pure sense of peace that surpasses understanding when we feel stable and safe. Our worst fears disappear in the security of abiding the law of the land for all people.

Everything plays a pivotal role in experiencing the love and affection from our family, friends, and working environment. The feeling of love and belongingness fulfills every desire to elevate to the next step of life.

Epiphany:
An Embodiment of Doubt

There is a dominant force within affirmations to make them work on our behalf. Affirmations will strategize our greatness into a beacon of eternal hope. "People can get many good things by the words they say."~ Proverbs 12:4

Our mind tends to reflect on all of the negative thoughts concerning ourselves; yet, we can negate our thinking by replacing those negative thoughts with real, active ones. It can stimulate wonders to our ego.

Every breath of life, each day, is another opportunity to conquer vast wealth. Empowering our frame of thinking will boost our reality into something magical. Decisions are very crucial to being in the right place, performing the right task, and within the divine hour.

The fear of the unknown can deter and deteriorate our strength. These concerns vividly paint traces of human errors, politics, evil, and confusion. There is one first mistake made by us or contributed by another. The actions can have an atrocious effect leading into adverse circumstances. Yes, we are human and are prone to making mistakes. Some are one problem away from a series of horrible situations as a domino effect.

The shortage of adequate resources can cause fear due to a lack of something such as, quality education due to racial barriers and financial means of providing the appropriate tools to equip our fearful mindsets. Fear may drive a person into another terrible factor, snatching away the sound mind we once had a long time ago. It will take perseverance to fight over fear, and strength to adapt and find alternative solutions to gain the proper outlets to compensate for lack of within our people.

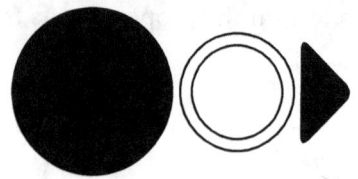

TREMAINE

"Excuse me, can you spare some change? I am trying to get something to eat."

Chuck began counting change, then bent over to give the woman spare dollars and coins.

"Here you go, here's a few dollars to buy a sandwich." Chuck stood there looking at Tremaine from head to toe, as she approached, thinking to himself *There she is. Ready to play dirty with me...just how I like it. Simone is so conservative with love making now since the pregnancy. Well, truth be told even before then, so a brother has needs.*

Tremaine walked up and said, "Hi, Sweetheart. Sorry, I am a few minutes late. Honey, you should have your key to the apartment on you, so you wouldn't have to wait outside."

He stood on the front door step piercing through her soul. "Baby, I know. You do know I would wait all day for you. I'll have a chance to see this lovely canvas."

As they passionately kissed, the homeless woman started to stare even harder. Tremaine unlocked the door to her apartment. She and Chuck rushed in and immediately started to make out on the floor.

Chuck's phone rang continuously. It was obvious that he would concentrate harder on what was in front of him. *Ring the alarm baby,* Tremaine thought to herself. Chuck reached over and cut the ringer off, mid-stroke. Tremaine was convinced his energy was electrifying as if he was a clone or something; because, his stamina tonight was out of this world.

Each time I hear your voice, I start to breathe again,

baby it's surreal and serene.

Each time I imagine your touch,

I arched my back

and pant for more caresses

of you in my dreams.

To have anything opposite,

like a long red stemmed rose

I would wither away and die.

This was their ritual three, sometimes four, days a week. It seemed they could never make it to the bedroom. They promised each other that they would try to work on it.

Chuck grabbed his phone to check the time and said, "Baby, it's almost one o'clock in the morning. I better get home." As he got up from the tangled living room furniture, he began throwing the couch pillows back into place. After grabbing his garments, he started putting his things back on. "You are home," Tremaine snarled. As he put his last shoe on, he reached over to give her one last hug and kiss, and said, "You know what I mean. See you soon, Darling. I love you."

At Last

At last, we finally cling together
like bread and butter.
Once upon a time our love was blind
from the sexual clutter.
Now I realize you are so anxious to try
so I thought if I gave you a sample
we could get by.
As far as I can see, I see us building our grounds
not one another ignoring each other's pleading sounds.
Time is on our side, if we only realize
how precious we are to one another.
Although if we can acknowledge it, we're
just two desperate doves in the sky,
mingling just to be.
And what an ugly way to be together yet
to not know the reason why.
Why are we together, finally, after all these years?
This is the question my heart cries.
So I don't know about you, partner
but I'm here for the long run to be there for many
dirty dancing moments orchestrated by the sun.

Epiphany:
Particles of Your Worth

Have you ever felt your knife was quite dull? Forcefully slicing the peppers and onions as you prepare your meal, you realize you must re-sharpen the knife, so that you can slice through the vegetables precisely and effortlessly. This is identical to our individual disposition at times. One day, I decided to grab a yummy cup of latte. I patronized one of our local food chains only to receive less than desirable service at the drive-thru window. Surely, the bad service influenced the taste of my mocha latte. Negative energy wrapped in a brand is not in the best interest of the company's reputation.

We can all use a self-image inspection. It can possibly spare us great regrets in the long term. The negative aura may stem from hurt, jealousy or unhappiness. Whatever the underlying cause, we must recognize and check our own, personal self-image and growth. Once we acknowledge the signs, our personal "service light" will alert us with different warnings.

Our interactions or first impressions will last longer than we can imagine. Whether a character reference in an elite organization, or a business transaction voting quorum, this can have a positive or negative impact on our daily lives. It also has the potential of affecting our family legacy.

Fine tuning our image is a positive habit to adapt. When we are aware of our self-worth, it can assist in eliminating the past failures. While, stimulating focus on your potential future in your daily interactions with others, always remember to ask yourself, "What type of particles am I?"

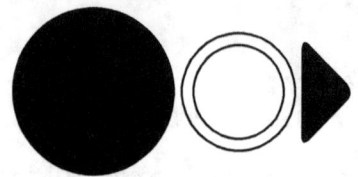

SIMONE

Simone's baby must have been screaming, "Feed me Seymour," while she was eating a bowl of cereal. He or she just wouldn't stop moving. As footsteps begin to draw near, the sound of keys rattling was followed by a deep raspy voice.

"Why are you still up? Are you still reading that pregnancy book?"

Simone gently placed the book on top of the bed. "What book? The What to Expect When You Suspect that Your Husband is Cheating book?"

"Simone, you knew you and I were having problems before you decided to get pregnant anyhow," Chuck said, boldly.

"Really, Chuck? Oh, I suppose it only took me to conceive a child, right?" Chuck sat on the chaise in front of the bed and began removing his shoes.

He asked, "What, are you joining the #MeToo movement now, seriously? Alright, do you really want to get down to it? How do I know that the baby is even mine?"

Simone replied, "I am not going there with you, as you fail to get me off track from where the hell have you been all night?"

Now shirtless, he stood up and headed in the direction of the master bathroom. Right before entering he stopped and looked at Simone.

"Listen, woman, I love you. I am tired. I just want to take a shower and get some sleep in the house. Last I checked, I am paying for it. I am coming from a very long day at work."

Simone stared at the ceiling, flabbergasted. "Oh, so I don't help with anything, right?"

"I didn't say that, Sweetheart," he said, as he stood there undressing. "I am saying Uber, Baby, ain't cutting it. Maintaining everything we got going on, let alone, another mouth to feed."

Epiphany: Complacent Love

Please don't spit in my face and tell me that it's raining. I ain't buying it. There are much needed, long overdue discoveries. The reality is, we spend seventy percent of our lives attempting to ensure others are comfortable around us. It only places a pause on our very own comfort level.

How much do we have to bend over backwards to allow an ungrateful human being to acknowledge and attempt to show a snippet of gratitude for our efforts? How can we become so desensitized to one another? The very ones who make individuals a priority in their lives are an afterthought of reflection with no direct action.

Excuse me, Mr. or Mrs. Complacent One, did you ever sit to think about others around you that choose to tolerate egotistical mannerisms? Yes, we are usually the ones that don't rain on your parade.

We usually take your feelings to heart and look out for your best interest in determining the proper time or place to explain why the parade was almost a disaster. The famous, "See what happened was..." scenario all circumvented due to our thoughtfulness and eagerness to be in your corner and not on the opponent's side. We conform to areas and energies without reconstructing it to suit our identity. We shouldn't have to give instructions to every single person on how to be compassionate. From this day forward, let us not put our happiness on the "it can wait" shelf. We will wear it on our sleeves while doing the most unselfish act for others. This gesture is how complacency meets *hit the dirt buster* live and in color.

Busy Bee

Busy bee work so hard and diligently
left right, left right
gliding from daisy to lily.
So many chores, so little time
to finish their tasks
before the sunset takes over the mask.

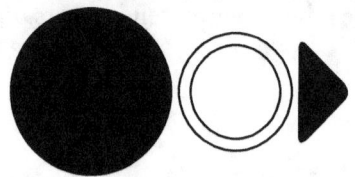

PENELOPE

At seven o'clock in the morning, Penelope was sitting inside her 2017 black Hyundai Elantra. It was a ritual, prior to her walking into work, to speak affirmations sitting inside the car. Penelope's mantra today would be to choose the right thoughts. "I am in control of what I allow to prance through my mind. My think tank will be clear from cluttered, unnecessary negativity. I will begin to reflect on the potential that I have inside. Therefore, I will refrain from entertaining what others think of who I am and what I should become in this world. I am a living masterpiece, beautifully sculpted for all to see and bear witness of the fruits I will continue to produce. I will intentionally place people around me who have already been through something. I won't allow people to speak into my life who haven't been through anything. My enemies may plot against me and attempt to discourage my will to succeed. I will not give in. I will not water or feed into the bullshit. I refuse to allow toxic to grow inside of me. Yes, I am mentally conscious or unconsciously programming my mind to believe in these positive affirmations. My complete desires are on the way to me. I believe everything I long for will equally long for me."

Penelope exited the car and walked across the parking lot, approaching the huge double glass doors to enter the doom of hell, better known as, her new j-o-b.

As she approached her cubicle, she noticed a stack of papers waiting for her to address. Penelope began to check her email and noticed a message from Phil, an old co-worker, that stated that his boss, Hillary, informed him that she knew Penelope's new boss, Rasputia, very well. Although, the crazy part was, Penelope didn't know anyone here named Rasputia.

It struck as quite odd. She didn't have a working relationship with Hillary at her prior place of employment. Hillary sounded suspicious with this, like she gave Phil a bone to carry. Penelope knew Hillary's interest about this new job's responsibilities wasn't genuine. Her stomach began to tighten while feeling dreadful inside her gut. So, she placed one hand around her stomach and the other over her heart and chanted, "I am remarkable, and I approve of myself and feel great about myself. I re-programmed my mind while taking a long deep breath. It does not matter what others think. What truly matters is how I react and what I believe to be factual."

Penelope's team mate, Chutney, a petite Iranian woman who was very intelligent with a pleasant personality, walked by on her way down the hallway and greeted Penelope's cubicle mate.. Moments later, there was an awful smell of dead human feces and dried sautéed onions with sushi lingering, and a mix of floral perfume. It was unbearable to the point that there was no way Penelope could refrain from screaming at the top of her lungs. She attempted to hold her damn breath, trying to wait it out until the invaded fumes disappeared. Penelope almost blacked out, to say the least. It never failed when Chutney was present. It seemed the fumes would slowly creep into the room as it darkened somehow, until moments after she left the room. Then, there was a beacon of light.

Hours later, Penelope overheard her name from across the room by her immediate supervisor, Lucinda. She informed Penelope that her current position would immediately report to Rasputia, who was currently on sick leave for a month. The same name was just referenced in Penelope's email a couple of hours prior. She knew something didn't feel right about it. While Penelope began to go through boxes of manual documents at her desk, the phone started to vibrate. It was a collect call from her estranged husband, Jeff.

Everything had been perfect for Penelope and Jeff. They had just moved into a lease to own property. It was a beautiful dream home with high vaulted tray ceilings, marble countertops, and ceramic tiles throughout. The master bedroom was large enough for a studio apartment with a spacious walk-in closet, and the bathroom had its very own jacuzzi with jets installed to top things off. Life was going as planned for the couple; until Jeff was incarcerated in the Augusta Correctional Center in the state of Virginia. He's in there for child support, which led to a DUI, violation of probation, and a get rich scheme gone wrong. He has been incarcerated now for over five months for violating a three year probation. The scheme was dealing with unclaimed automotive parts.

Recently, Jeff was hospitalized from transmitting a deadly infection called MRSA, or staphylococcus infection, inside prison confines. He underwent an emergency surgery to extract flesh. The deadly fungus was found spreading in between his genital area. If untreated, it could become deadly by invading one's bloodstream and eventually eating the tissue. Not addressing this immediately means that it could spread in communicable, unclean surroundings such as a hospital or incarcerated facilities. Penelope strongly believed a systematic approach for saving lives to halt the spread of this infection can be ideal. It can be principles established by being made aware that the problem exists to make better processes. The leadership needs to establish a goal of creating good healthcare practices through system thinking and eliminating the blame and finding permanent solutions. They must see things differently through new eyes to better serve the client as opposed to governing themselves. The support staff is setup to make human errors due to stress and unrealistic expectations.

Penelope answered the phone, "Hi, Honey!"

Jeff replied, "Baby, it's so good to hear your. Baby, I miss you."

Penelope smiled as she said, "I miss you also, Darling. You won't believe the craziest thing just happened to me; however, I don't know what it all means just yet. How can I explain it?"

"What happened?" Jeff asked.

Penelope sat at her cubicle multitasking and counting the stacks of sorted manuals to verify the total amount. Sheconsistently displayed her loving mannerisms to Jeff, even during their estranged relationship. She felt responsible for being his beacon of light while he was incarcerated. So, she continued to be a supportive partner.

"I know you have warned me on several occasions that working for our people was a recipe for disaster," she said. "Surely, there's bound to be drama somewhere. Folks envy you or will throw you under the bus trying to get to the top."

Jeff responded, "Just keep your head up baby girl, it will get better. Sweetheart, I need to get tuna, chili, drinks and Little Debbie snacks. Can you put some money in my commissary?" "Yes, Darling, of course I will add money to your commissary. I'll do my best. I will get it done during my hour for lunch," she told him. Then, the operator's voice interrupted to prompt them to end the call because their allotted time had expired.

Laundry

Shades of blue, red, black piled in a clutter
along with a pair of polyester slacks,
and a pair of kitchen mittens
stained with butter.
Yet, it all belongs to me.
No matter how my dirty laundry appears to be,
it may be a sight for sore eyes to see.
Blemished pieces and garments, some try to interpret
you by the load you may be carrying.
So, what are you carrying today?
For the world is anxious to know.
Always remember folks try to judge you, be the color of your clothes.
Yet, it is kind of delirious how one interprets someone's outer
appearance.

Stay woke. There are times in our lives when you must refuse what you see with your eyes or even hear with your own ears. You must evaluate everyone, especially the ones in your circle...family, friends, foe. Screening everyone will attest to their readiness in taking directives. Then, we can discover their lack and build them in achieving to develop it.

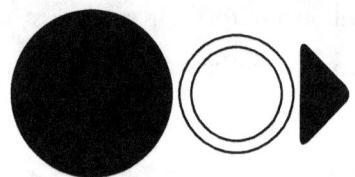

GIGI

The spa's ambience renewed Gigi throughout her session. The tranquil space was so inviting. As soon as you walked in, there was a vibrant splash of warm color from the bouquet of flowers sitting on the countertop. The aromas in the place exquisitely trespassed her senses to engage in the peacefulness without comprehension. The whole place seems so clean with white and neutrals throughout the space. Gigi imagined herself off the Atlantic Ocean near Casablanca, Morocco with surprising fluorescent lighting and unique architectural designs in the background. She was totally enjoying the smell of lavender and serene sounds of the waterfall from the tall melodic fountain. The soothing sounds persuaded Gigi to think of deep ocean waves crashing against the shore.

As the receptionist approached to greet Gigi, she offered a glass of natural spring water infused with lime and mint along with a pair of comfy slippers and a fluffy robe to change into.

On the counter top, there was a warm towel or two placed neatly in a heart shape. Gigi anticipated what was next from the therapist, in hopes of melting away all her stress, and most importantly, to create the perfect mood.

And, then, walked in her assigned massage therapist for today, Patty. And the sounds of crickets began to lurk along with a pure smell of tart shit, and old spearmint gum steaming from Patty's mouth as she spoke. Ironically, she greeted her and began to start on the upper back. A deep tissue massage is just what she needed.

"Hello, are you comfortable?" she asked. It took every strength of her being to say, "Sure," because Gigi really wanted to say, "Most definitely, until you walked in."

"Yes I am," she replied.

It never failed, she always had more than an ear full to tell about her relationship problems. Gigi don't have any sob stories of her own or to share from family and friends even. She had been bamboozled. Gigi thought this place was a magical, healthy and stress-free environment. Truth is, it's the home of Medusa! She should be paying her for the damn massage, hell.

Epiphany:
Uninvited Stupidity!

Maybe only we can take away the time when our mistakes were on display in front of several bystanders to witness. The way we handle the uh-oh's or intentional human glitches will often deter us from the overall rewards. Sometimes, we place ourselves in the wrong environments. When they are accurate, then there is no arrival because we just belong. The very moment we are not missed by folks, it creates certain internal anxieties. Our calling can be very vital to our planned assignment. As we verify the identity of our enemies, we are closer to wisdom. Assignments always contain enemies. We must diligently decipher through the righteous or unrighteous assignments. Enemies are invitations to successes nearby. No interference can lead to idle actions towards attaining goals. Unhandled associations of trapped stupidity will consume and hinder us from greater expectations. The child who treats his or her parents the best is the most intelligent person in the whole world. Crying for wisdom will put us closer to our dreams. A lifestyle of seeking challenges to grant advancement towards identifying difference in right and wrong. Every human being on earth is not equal. There are some people who feed our gifts. Everyone is an arrangement to our future or past. What are some of the indicators? There are people in our lives who need us to live. There are some who genuinely believe in our successes and bright futures ahead. Faith supersedes most things because it causes supernatural experiences larger than our imagination. Donations, forgiveness and volunteering are examples of seeds. As we evaluate our uninvited stupidity together, let's keep these things in our perspective.

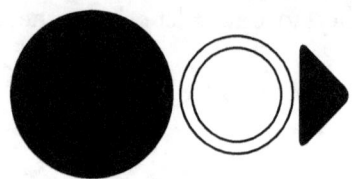

GIGI

The very large, custom made sliding chestnut door seemed heavy. It took so long for the unknown person on the opposite side to enter. While Gigi was being guided by Patty from the therapy area, passt the reception lobby and pedicure station area, into the sauna, Simone walked in. It was very obvious Gigi was thankful to see Simone arrived just in time to rescue her!

"Simone, I am so happy to see you. I could kiss you right now!" she exclaimed.

Simone shook her head in excitement for this precious time to unwind.

"See here, I am so looking forward to this sauna. I choose not to even imagine it right now," Simone replied.

Gigi hadn't seen Simone in about two weeks, so they had a bunch of catching up to do indeed. Patty, the therapist, prepared to leave. "Thank you, Ms. Gigi," she said. "Enjoy your next experience."

"Uh huh. Yes, say no more," Gigi said as she pushed Simone in the direction toward the entrance, with her eyes zoned ahead to free herself from the trauma she had experienced in the other room with Patty.

Gigi asked Simone, "What's going on with you today?"

Epiphany:
The Philosophy of Elevated Chatter

There exists endless tests in our lifetime. Weightless cheers and shout outs come in all shapes and sizes. Stingy cheerleaders are always present in your face. There are many types of people that are spoilers, whiners, and dreamers. The spoilers are mainly chatter boxes gone wild, trying to stay relevant in the recent activities true or false.

Whiners have a negative tone on everything; firsthand with pessimistic views on life and others around them. Our dreamers are very peculiar people because they create fairytale environments to benefit their truths from their romanticized dreams. Investment in learning is essential to self-improvement. We always face two choices...to win or lose. The pursuit of knowledge has defined our personal blueprint.

Once we identify our mentor, it allows us to learn through another individual's pain. We can consider this process as identified knowledge mapping, because no one likes to be defeated - these self-inflicted opportunities for growth through our wrestled fears of failure. You are gorgeously made and so deserving of a winning story. We must always remember to place good vibes out into the universe. Our primary objective is to seek eternal rewards in every battle.

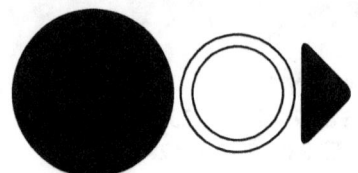

GIGI

"Charles and I are crumbling down," Simone said.

"No, Simone, not like the London Bridge!"

"I am afraid so. Piece by piece. And, do you want to know the scary part? I have no control over the devastation it's going to create for us."

"Well, my heart goes out to you two, Simone. I mean the baby doesn't need anymore stress."

Simone optimistically replied, "No, this heat is giving me life right now."

Gigi concurred, "Yes! Come on heat shock proteins!"

Simone chuckled. "You know what? Not today."

"See, there's that smile!"

Simone asked, "So, how did it go with the intervention on the homeless girl you mentioned? You know, the one that has a drug problem? Were you able to convince her to seek help, like counseling or check into a safe house or rehab facility?"

Gigi responds, "Yeah, it's been weighing on my conscience like a ton of bricks. I have talked to my psychologist friend about considering taking her as a new client. I haven't seen her just yet. I plan to encourage her to not give up."

"Good for you. That's noble of you to care, Gigi."

Gigi replied, "Well, technically she is still a minor for goodness sake."

"Now, I can't imagine a mother or father disowning their flesh and blood, then leaving them out in a cruel world to survive alone."

Gigi began to shake her head in agreement as she said, "We must take responsibility and help each other. This place is a cruel place. It will chew you up and spit you out quick. "

Simone agreed. "I am at a place in time where I am prepared to protect my unborn creation alone to prevent anything like that from happening, so I should get Simone together fast. I see evidence, directly from Charles, constantly reminding me our problems are real, daily."

"Simone, what are you talking about?"

"Gigi, he is beginning to belittle my contributions to the household, like my job is a non-factor. Also, he makes it seem like I don't have a voice. It's very hurtful."

"What? I'm so sorry, girl."

"Yes, we are in a very dark place. I am so close to delivering this child and getting stronger. Soon, I can plan a life without him in it."

"Girl, are you considering giving up on your marriage? Girl, don't do it. Fight, Simone. You must fight."

"I'm trying; yet, I don't want to fight for this all alone. Charles and I have survived a lot of storms. This is not the first one. Either way, I would have remained steadfast and stood by him throughout his faults. Even during his drug usage, or the time I caught him at a hotel with a white woman. Even caught this woman driving the vehicle I was paying the car note for. I can recall the white trash leaving behind her purse, then, out of curiosity, my ass wanted to know her identity, only to find a sketching of the devil on a blank sheet of paper first."

"Wait a minute, what did you just say? Did you meet Lucifer, Simone?"

"Yes, it seemed that way, because I was looking for her ID or driver's license. Instead, I found a sketching of the devil sketched with a pencil first. It was then that I realized that this is spiritual warfare. It was not my battle to fight anymore. I surpassed that heartache only to end up laying in the hospital bed losing our first child, as he looked me in my eyes with rage and anger and told me the baby wasn't his. I even supported him through his quest to get clean from drugs that led to more infidelity with the married blue tongue aka Jezebel."

Epiphany: Donors of Repetitive Character Assassination

How many times have you been a victim to someone damaging your image? Due to the family Thanksgiving festivities, all the bells and whistles were seen, yet, to find grandmother's heirloom glass pitcher broken. Once aunts and uncles rush in to learn what has happened, your best cousin, little Johnnie, points the blame at you when, in fact, he did it accidentally.

It only takes one utter of dismay to cause disappointment, fear, and pain to bestow on the accused victim. There was something or someone who triggered a reason to be envious and judgmental. These things can only stem from desperate attention seeking bullies, exaggerated half-truths, and actively engaged rumors.

We can embrace the ramifications behind targeted wounds by damage control efforts, such as, renouncing their connection. Also, we can acknowledge all bystanders affected by the murderous attacks are apologetic; sympathy for witnessing the donor's cowardly acts. The justified reasons for their discredited attempts are because, initially, they lack support and have been rejected by their family and community.

A donor of repetitive character assassination is a form of bullying based on several reasons, such as, not being approved for the requested promotion and hating on your co-worker's accomplishment in a lateral move. These donors long to possess the gifts and talents the accused victim possesses. It is the fuel behind the already blazing fire to discredit the targeted victim's influence and credibility.

We all have a role to play in a society that we all share. We can think of exciting ways to ignite love and admiration in the hearts of all our children. They may find the love and support at home and around their community to be a positive contributor to the whole picture in our society, and not an inhibitor. This movement can become a bandwagon effect when we all discover the value in showing compassion to one another. These are the real reasons to be thankful for the simple things that will last over a lifetime.

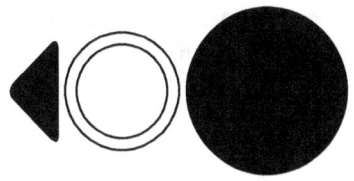

GIGI

Simone continued with her story "She attempted to sabotage our marriage by money, and out of town bike trips with their biker crew. They even got matching his and hers tattoos, dared to make a flimsy sexual video in the middle of the woods butt ass naked, while she was giving him fellatio in broad daylight. I *survived*. I survived her attempts of assassinating my character by threatening texts and calls accusing me of sleeping with his close friend to brainwash him. He even arranged for the serpent-like tramp to come to our home and pick him up. Baby, when I tell you, I looked over all of it and entirely forgave him."

"Well, maybe you should seek marital counseling from your pastor, Simone."

Simone replied, "I don't think it will do any good because he has accused the pastor and I of having a fling!" Gigi began to shake her head in disbelief while panting for air. They both sat there dripping in sweat, shredding away dreadful toxins.

Simone reached down to grab her towel. "Listen, God chooses not to fix it now, Gigi. I don't want it."

"You're right. I am so sorry, Simone. Although, it's refreshing to learn, you have grown to know your infinite worth and the value you have in this world."

They began to hug as the beeper chimed, indicating their paid session had ended.

Epiphany: Anybody Have a Heart?

There is still a heart that is forever caring in all its beings. There should be human lives that speak life in other living creatures. We live in a world full of "no she didn't" and "oh my gosh, look at her butt," when we don't take the time out to study the value added.

Society channels our emotions to a competitive mockery of ill-will, envious, fantasized false hopes. We can all attest to reading between all the current propaganda to evaluate the more delicate things such as, pursuing our dreams, being accountable for our carbon footprints and whether we speak to Ms. Sue in the grocery store or pretend to walk past without any shame.

All human lives play vital roles in what the future will bring. How it will be remembered lies in our very hands. We can pay it forward to pass on the feeling of love in our hearts and wisdom in our minds. The past is a constant reminder that we are so much more than our obstacles because we are a victorious living being.

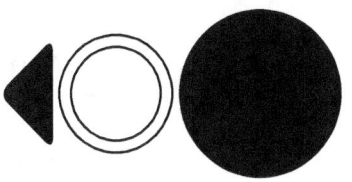

CHLOE

The darkness outweighed the light, and the only signs of it came from the piercing stars above. *Why are we running in the middle of the woods at night in fear? Who are we running away from exactly?* Chloe laid in her bed panicking, drenched in sweat. She kept revisiting the same horrible nightmare from her youth like it just happened yesterday. She had never been more scared in a dream compared to this one. Chloe knew she had to snap out of this before she went insane.

Epiphany: An Ocean of Dreams!

Throughout life, we tend to have limited visions of our lives, previewed through dreams. It gives us a determination to translate what it means. There are resource materials that provide persuasive judgments on what our ideas detail.

They never encountered the close, real life experience of vivid reenactment. There are those dreams that leave your heart panting and gasping for air once awaken. The moments when you rush out of your bed and feel it is the next day! You are late for work only to realize it is only late in the evening. Yes, I have been there and done that several times.

The embarrassment of how silly you were and how real it seemed is very troublesome. Our lost dreams are voices in our mind which are waiting to be discovered and made a reality through sound judgment and dedication. We seek to account for the many tangible manifestations, awkward compassion over the many talents and properties that we possess.

The lost voices depicted in our dreams are pieces to life's puzzle of success. Some of us have witnessed our dreams becoming a reality through negative or positive events. Our goals can linger into our thoughts and fuel our intuition. It helps deter harmfully, or confirm great things on the horizon for us when we keep our faith. A tangible manifestation of our steadfastness makes everything sweeter than before. We are more appreciative of the simple things that we never ask to receive. Our quality of life increases positively because of our determination to build our dreams into reality.

Many individuals along the way may have provided awkward compassion towards us on this journey. Their struggle to see past their shortcomings or current obstacles motivates their awkwardness towards our happiness. We all must remain good stewards of the many gifts and talents we all possess. They are loaned to us in this lifetime to assist us in helping others to attain the knowledge of interpreting their dreams.

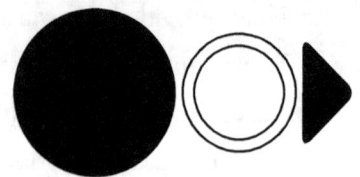

CHLOE

Dr. Olay recommended when that happens, Chloe must try to change her thought patterns to something uplifting to prevent depression relapse. She suggested that she read her daily devotion from Bible study or pick up an inspirational book to clear her thoughts. What did seem to help for Chloe, though, was text messages from Mr. Travis Garnett. His texts provoked deep, intimate thoughts about him, which automatically reduced her anxiety level.

Chloe and Travis had grown to know each other over the past two months . They worked out three days a week in person, and once through Skype or live video chatting to accomplish her fitness goals. He seemed to be a very talented trainer. Chloe began to discover Travis' fit physique while spending more time together.

So far, her waistline had diminished by three inches; even her buttocks had started to lift. Chloe noticed her favorite frequently worn old, torn jeans didn't cling to her curves anymore. Oddly, Chloe primped in the mirror more frequently, trying new hair and make-up tips to enhance her beauty. She had even started to sleep longer and not wake up in the middle of the night from the nightmares.

Chloe and Travis had a private Facetime session, and surprisingly Travis expressed an interest in getting to know Chloe better. Flattered, Chloe replied, "Surely you can have any girl you want."

Travis replied, "I want you."

"How do you know you want me?"

"The very first moment I saw you, I envisioned you by my side, as my queen."

"Go on," Chloe said, blushing.

"And after discovering I had the opportunity to spend more time with you, I knew it was only a matter of time."

"Well, hopefully, time will be on our side," Chloe said, as she continued her last set of mountain climber exercises, facing him in a pair of fitted black biker shorts and a fuchsia sports bra. He had VIP access to observe up close.

The Intellectual Virus

*Deadly potent intellect
spreads frightful calm with smooth dialect.
Makes me tremble, yet,
I can't regret
the fortune of being in tuned to you.
Incurable unknown call
as I attempt to keep up with your intimate dialogue.
Damn he's deep
blue seas of mystery
I wonder if he's really digging me?
I mean, this knowledge could be toxic
until it wipes out the entire selected billion.
Damn, I can't be getting weak.
This deadly potent intellect
is putting me out of my misery.
It's getting dark and my heart
is fading softly. Let me be
Calm, smooth with dialect.
I'm beginning to get my pulse back
So I continue to give you my convo of my steelo.
We continue to flow strong.
I'm digging you and now you dig me while the clock
continues to tick tock on.
My heartbeat is racing,
no time for contemplating it seems.
Is there a cure for this brain disease?
That's killing me, or it's something that I just perceived?*

Front stage passes granted an exclusive showing of the girls up close and personal, with cleavage glistening from the amount of sweat dripping from working out. Travis was mesmerized staring at her, and he continued to give encouraging words as Chloe suddenly worked even harder from the adrenaline inspired by their heated discovery of attraction for each other.

"You are doing fantastic, Baby Girl."

"Thank you! I owe it all to you, Travis."

Travis replied, "Well, you keep this going and you'll reach your personal fitness goals in no time."

"I don't know how to thank you enough."

"Listen, my pleasure. I am heading out to a late session, so I must get going. You're more than welcome to join me one day...on your off day, of course."

Cyber Love

You've got mail.
It reads, "Hi love, you are so beautiful.
Can I get some of your time?"
As I read between the lines,
can I call you? He asked
smooth calm and relaxed
as I carefully examined the
photo attached.
Damn, He looks good,
at least that's what it seems.
What does it mean?
I wonder if he copied someone else's identity?
Hey, there are plenty of internet freaks,
let me contemplate and rethink.

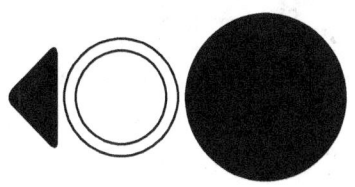

DR. ANASTASIA OLAY

The anticipation of meeting this young woman was quite intense, considering that Dr. Olay was doing something rare by going to her in her element. She was not in her office; instead, she was driving into the heart of the south-side of the city while Waze directed her toward the area, in search of this young lady named Katina Rozell. Dr. Olay arrived at the location and began to walk alongside the narrow sidewalk. The peddlers sensed she was far from the yellow brick road, portraying her as Dorothy from The Wizard of Oz. Dr. Olay began to question why in the world she agreed to this foolishness. Oh yeah, it was a substantial amount of cash Gigi gave to her as a deposit for this pursuit.

The thought of what the remaining amount would be after this counseling session ended eased Dr. Olay's anxiety just a tad. Surely it motivated her as she anxiously chuckled internally. Dr. Olay approached a woman fitting Katina's description, which Gigi had described over the phone. Gigi said that she was tall, slender, with natural hair and robust cheekbones. She called out Katina's name, hoping she would answer, but no response. A woman that fit her description asked a nearby stranger walking by, "Hey, you got a Lucy?"

The pedestrian answered, "No." Dr. Olay loudly called out to her again. Katina looked up from her slumber and attempted to figure out Dr. Olay's identity.

She was laying on the side of a red brick graffiti wall, which appeared to have gang signs spray painted across the side of the old vandalized building. Her belongings were kept in a large trash bag filled with clothes.

"Hi, Katina, my name is Anastasia. Gigi's friend. She wanted me to come by and meet you." Katina's eyes stretched wide as she said, "Gigi? Yea, I know her. I haven't seen her this week." Dr. Olay replied, " She told me to let you know she will see you soon."

"Oh okay.

Dr. Olay asked,"Katina, would you like to go?"

"Go where?" Katrina asked, as she looked around at her surroundings. It was as if she was expecting someone to walk up at any moment.

Dr. Olay replied, "How about we go and grab a bite to eat? Do you feel ok about that? I mean if you are expecting someone, then I understand."

Katina began to ponder as she paused and looked around. "Oh, okay. I guess that will be ok."

Dr. Olay put both hands together. "Great, there's a charming southern cuisine bistro a few blocks away from here, and my car is right around the corner," she said.

Southern Girl

I am a southern girl
Don't be surprised
by my fiercely disguise
just recognize
I'm not an ordinary broad.
I have a smooth, sleek, southern drawl
Men's dig my style.
Some run to my presence and some may crawl.

As the waiter guided us to our seat, Katina asked, "Excuse me, where's the restroom?"

The waitress replied, "It's on the right, to your very back."

Katina proceeded to get up as Dr. Olay's phone rang. It was Gigi. As Katina walked away heading towards the restroom, Dr. Olay picked up to answer the phone call.

"Hi, girl. Katina and I just arrived at a small bistro. I must make it quick. She just stepped away to the ladies room."

. "Listen, Tasia, go slow with her. The girl is fragile," Gigi told her.

"I mean, Gigi, you haven't given me anything to work with in the first place. Now, she's fragile? What is that supposed to mean exactly?"

Gigi explained, "Well, what I do know is that Katina was in a safe house due to her family disowning her at an early age. Then, she became involved in a very dysfunctional, toxic relationship with her boyfriend at the time, who introduced her to drugs like opioids, and manipulated her into being involved in sex trafficking. That's what I know!"

"Oh Lord, now you tell me? Did you once think I would've appreciated this information prior to this very MOMENT?"

"Well, I didn't want you to change your mind and give up on her. So many people have turned their backs on the poor girl!"

"Well she's walking back I got to go. And, Gigi, you owe me big time."

Epiphany: Consciously Speaking in a Lifetime!

In a blink of an eye, all things can be made anew, depending on your perception of how things appear. Optical illusions are very intriguing because it allows the mind to consider the limitless possibilities. Have you ever taken a road trip on a beautiful countryside, and as you are traveling from a far distance, there is an illusion of a puddle of water or mass in the middle of the road; but it disappears from your view the closer you get to the area where it once appeared to be?

Even as you are approaching the hillside, there is a blockage to your view in the natural realm. Have you ever thought about the drawings of different objects in one illustration to determine which you interpret or see first? We, as a people, are accustomed to certain types of unknowns.

There are things in our lifetime that will appear before us, and we see them for what they are at that moment. Over time, the things we have collected will change, and we are left to fit the pieces together again, such as favorite possessions, loved ones, and different circumstances.

Our family can be contributors when it comes to being introduced to strangers. They tend to list all our talents and gifts before allowing the person to find out.

It allows our loved ones a sense of pride to flaunt the level of education, or a better lifestyle or career. We must set us apart from the common folk right out the door. It can leave a sense of bragging rights, which, sometimes, parents should be allowed in individual settings. Rather than letting your audience to genuinely inquire about you than to provide a human manual of unwanted accolades.

Sometimes we have a vain outlook on material things. We use favorite possessions, such as money, cars, clothes or homes to beautify us, and allow it to become a part of what represents us. It appears these material things provide a sense of security in a particular area that we lack. Favorite possessions can alter our image in another light to circumvent the actual reality of who we are now. In an instance, or over time, those favorite possessions, which we cling on to, can be taken from us at any moment. Thus, leaving us as whom we are in the first place.

Different circumstances allow us to see things for what they really are. We are trained to provide a 1 to 2-minute alleviated pitch of who we are in our own words. Oppositely, when we go through different comfortable or uncomfortable situations, it allows us to determine a person for who they intend to be, based on how they handle different circumstances.

In a lifetime, our consciousness describes our inner being for us; so, let's stop wasting time on how we want others to perceive us to be, when all along, the underlying surface shows itself through our favorite possessions, loved ones, and different circumstances.

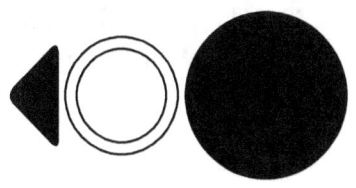

DR. ANASTASIA OLAY

Katina returned and sat down before jumping right in. , "So what is it that you want from me?" she asked.

"No, I don't want anything...just to offer you dinner and to introduce myself to you. As I said before, I am a friend of Gigi and she mentioned that you are an extraordinary person to her. She seemed to feel you, and I need to discuss some things." Dr. Olay took a sip of her large sweet maple cane tea, in a mason jar, with a lime and mint attached.

Katina replied, "Discuss? Discuss what? Look, lady, I don't know anything. I'm just out here surviving."

Dr. Olay placed her glass tumbler down on the granite charcoal table top, and said, "Well, for starters, how does a beautiful young lady end up living on the side of the street? Do you have anywhere to go?"

Katina looked around and shook her head. "You wanna know how? Well, it's easy; especially when your flesh and blood does not care about you. You see, I had to grow up quick. In and out of foster care until I aged out."

"You seem very wise for your age. So, you weren't prepared for transitioning. I can understand how vulnerable you were at that stage in life. So, where did you go when you reached eighteen? Did you finish school?"

"No, I had a fast life. They didn't care if I went to school."

"Fast, in what way?"

"I was homeless after they kicked me out."

"Excuse me, are you ready to place your order?" The waitress disrupted the moment.

"Yes, I'll have the shrimp and grits and a side of kale chips."

"And for you ma'am?"

"Oh, uhm, I don't..."

"She'll have the same."

"Ok, your order will be right up."

"Thank you."

Anastasia watched the waitress walk away from their table then turned back to Katrina. "I hope you didn't mind. I think you would enjoy this dish. It's their specialty," she said.

"It's cool," Katina said, and smiled with relief.

"Thank you for deciding to come out and have dinner with me. What were you saying about fast? You mean you ran track in high school?"

Katina looked amused. "No, I was introduced to drugs early to numb my pain and disappointment."

The server approached. "Two orders of shrimp & grits?"

"Yes, please."

"Would you care for any condiments or anything?"

"No, thank you."

The server replied, "Enjoy."

As Dr. Olay watched the server walk away, she realized she could really enjoy an alcoholic beverage to forget about current baggage at that very moment.

"I see. What type of drugs? Marijuana?"

Katina began to eat while attempting to respond to the question.

"Oh, *heroin, Vicodin, Morphine, Percocet, Oxycodone*. You name it, I did it." Saddened with disbelief, Dr. Olay asked, "How do you get access to something like that at such a young age?"

"My boyfriend who I saw at the time. He was older than me, so he would supply gifts to me on a regular to spoil me."

Dr. Olay asked, "With drugs?"

"I guess you can say that. Mostly candy; except he would give them to me as a reward. Listen, I better get going. I know they have been looking for me." Katina got up and began to leave.

Dr. Olay said, "Well, wait, let me take you home. I mean, back to where we met."

"No, it's ok, I need the air."

"Katina, did you know the meaning of your name is *pure*?"

Katina paused with curiosity and replied, "No I didn't know that."

Dr. Olay proceeded "Yes, therefore it means you are free from any contamination, and that you are beautiful and no one compares to you. Where you are does not define who you truly are. It was so nice meeting you. Maybe we can do this again real soon."

"No, I'd rather not. Everyone I get attached to usually ends up walking out, so I'm a natural loner."

Dr. Olay reached into her purse, pulled out her business card and handed it to Katina. Katina read it aloud. "Doctor Anastasia."

"It's just a title. My dear friends call me Tasia."

Katina replied, "Tasia? Ok, I better get going."

"Katina, I am here to sincerely express to you that I hope that you grow to know your infinite worth and the value you have in this thing called life."

As she began to walk out, leaving the restaurant, she threw her hand up, saying goodbye.

"Waiter, may I have my check and a to-go box, please?"

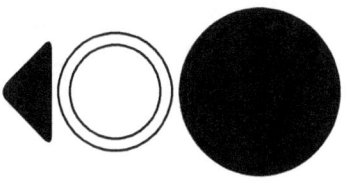

INTRODUCTION TO RIKA'S EPIPHANIES

Self-validation is necessary to fully discover one's true self. The actualization of becoming more of one's full potential, what you stand for, and how you love; and acknowledging the steps during the process. This process of discovery takes place through small or grand ideas or even big or small actions. The act of carrying something out through words or actions about something or someone. One's perception of thought should be valued in every situation due to efforts put forth in making it a reality in the first place. We must take the time to capture my ideas of opinion based on my experiences captured in these outlined epiphanies. These short stories can be useful in so many ways during your time here on earth. These epiphanies happened throughout the course of my life. There were periods of isolation, brokenheartedness and confusion about the world we cohabitate and share together. It is a reference of various highlighted aha moments of emotions experienced throughout my life which inspired the many topics. Hopefully, the information inspires you to consider another perspective on events or behaviors we may have encountered in some aspects of our lives.

Epiphany:
Evidence of Acid Tears!

How does one pick up the shattered pieces to mend things back together again? Through our evidence of coping, people gain respect for you through the process of tears.

The evidence of acid tears is found in ransomed visions, defeated feelings in the circumference of our problems. What would make your tears feel like acid because the pain irritates our heart and inflames our very soul?

Defeated feelings cause our red swollen eyes to visualize multiple problems. There are painful marks engraved permanently in our memories. The many ransomed visions of history have blocked our vision of our current position and future destiny. We must reconstruct our memories to support us in visualizing our bright future by placing a blazing torch beside our feet.

The circumference of our problems is not what it seems. We must be careful not to tamper with and hide our evidence of acid tears. These experiences help to balance things through diligent process by becoming a part of our plan to succeed.

Reflecting on the memories and reasons behind the tears will eventually lead to healing and progression. Ransomed visions can sometimes cause hurt and disappointment. We must possess the creed of hope in humanity. Defeated feelings possess the drive to overcome the circumference of our problems.

Precisely yours

Precisely what would you think if I told you,
"The sky is purple today."
Maybe it could be unlikely
to be true, based on what purple
skies mean to you.
To me, it means
that it's not how it appears to be
it seems.
A lovely person could be dreadful and unbearable to his
loved ones,
yet appears fun.
Now precisely or it's highly unlikely to be precisely.

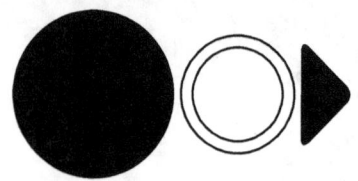

TREMAINE

It was Tremaine's baby's birthday. She had anticipated on making it rain! Ah ah ah! She put the last touches on the Portobello mushrooms, stuffed with kale, red onions, red and green peppers, chopped walnuts, and cooked quinoa, accompanied by a side dish of sautéed zucchini, golden onion rings, fresh cucumbers, olives, tomatoes and red onion atop a salad, infused with a lime juice seasoning finished with sprinkled hemp seeds.

She topped it off and put a foot in it with her version of ice cream made from almond milk and bananas with mixed berries for texture; coupled with a nice bottle of room temperature Eternal spring water *fit for a King*.

He should be walking through these doors any minute now, Tremaine thought. After their nutritious meal, she imagined seeing the expression on his face. Tremaine anticipated the excitement prior to the grand surprise visit to the strip club for him.

The keys rattled as the door opened like clockwork. Tremaine primped in the mirror for the last check on her fine self, as she chanted in her head, "Let the mojo begin. Go Tre, Go Tre!"

Temptation

As I caress the inner lips of my mouth
I start to ponder the length of my drought.
You don't miss your water
until your well runs dry.
Sometimes I contemplate even if I'm still alive
down there, quenching for every drop of moist
to satisfy my inner thirst.
No time to rehearse,
let it flow like the Nile River in Africa.
As I pant for more
water to cure.
My lasting drought is as dry as the
Sahara Desert on a hot blazing day.
One dose of pleasure
will keep me Kool-Aid.
To my mind, body, and spirit
let the chemical body fluids
flow as your sweet temple
loses control in it.
The greys in my hair are a symbol
of lost passion,
fantasizing day and night wondering
how long it will last?
Measuring every inch of my "well"
as I scream,

"All Hail" lives the king.
King of my tropical jungle
King ding a ling.

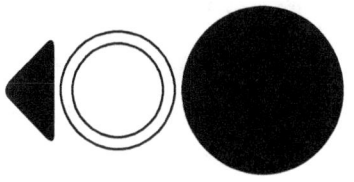

TREMAINE

"Hey, baby! Happy birthday! Today is your holiday, sweetheart."

Charles reached for a body hug. "Thank you, sweetie."

Tremaine flirtatiously replied, "Of course."

Charles whispered softly, "Listen...I..."

Tremaine ignored his faint voice and continued, "Of course dinner is ready for you. Let me cater to you, ok?"

Charles was hesitant about what he was about to share with her as he realized she had a grand finale waiting for him.

"Let's just relax. Take off your shoes and slide on these Persian, king size slippers I bought for you. King Jaffe Joffer, your dinner awaits!" As they chuckled with laughter, Tremaine guided him into the dining room, then took a seat at the dinner table for his feast.

Charles closed his eyes for a nanosecond then said, "Smells good, Baby."

Tremaine replied, "Why thank you, sweetheart. I simply want you to understand the infinite value of your own worth."

Fluttered, Charles asked, "What's on the menu?" as he began to clap his hands, then rub them together repeatedly.

Tremaine smiled. "We have a meal fit for a king."

"Oh, yeah we got some porterhouse steak, Baby?"

"Nooooo...We have Portobello mushrooms stuffed with kale, red onion, red and green peppers, chopped walnuts, cooked quinoa, a side dish of sautéed zucchini with golden onion rings and a fresh cucumbers, olives, tomatoes, and red onion salad infused in nice seasoning with lime juice."

Charles interrupted, "Well, Baby, I never told you this, but I have a nut allergy. I'm not too keen on olives, either."

"One day you will see the value in the meal that I prepared for you. I made all of it with love...straight from mother nature's kitchen, no genetically modified organisms in here. The devil is a liar!"

Epiphany: Tainted Dreams

The regulated sources of information pass judgments. These judgments are traces of exposing the realization of our worth in society. The inability to seek answers independently to verify our teaching can lead to inner untruths. It is our media outlets' proactive measures, and our elected leadership that will provide the resolutions instantly.

Our media outlets are the most powerful sources of influence today. The persuasiveness in strategized communication depicts biased scenarios. It can cause uproar contrary to peacefulness. The strength to discover the hard truths will create encouragement for others to become more proactive and not lax in the affairs of research. We have become accustomed to things being explained rather than asking the right questions to discover the whole truth about things in our society.

We all can monitor our lifestyle in such a way that it is not brainwashing our thoughts and preventing our critical listening skills. There are proactive measures to increase our diversified cultural behaviors. We can become superb listeners in every aspect of family, professional and citizenship. We are far from where we should be in the world we all share. It is things happening every day in our society that depict our shortcomings. The division of culture will create high tension and intense demonstrations of social injustice for all mankind. Our lack of respect for one another has exposed the truths of our reality. We must put peace and harmony back in the topics of our board meetings and judicial platforms. We have a right to act accordingly for our children's future to remain the great legacy of our ancestry.

It starts with an official acknowledgment, apology, and responsibility for the healing to begin in our world. It starts with the neighbor across the street or the person we pass in the grocery store. We all have a responsibility in understanding social cultural relations.

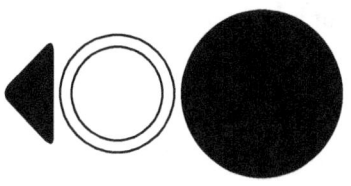

TREMAINE

"Thank you, Baby. I just want a simple T-bone steak, A1 sauce, corn on the cob, a baked potato with broccoli, and a slice of apple pie."

Tremaine replied, "If your slaughterhouse, genetically engineered, death food is what you're craving, then so be it."

He pleaded, "Baby, you know it's going to take time. A brother gotta have his meat now. Come on!"

"Ok, today I celebrate you, my king. We can place an order to pick up from the Waffle House, then head to our next surprise destination. I want you to understand, we are enslaved to believe in the consumption of meat in our diet. A plant based diet is ideal for consumption for a better quality of life. I understand we are addicted to eating animals, but there are major health risks inside these slaughterhouses. Kevin's Law is real; look it up for yourself. Every good thing belongs to you and the glory of liberty is rightfully yours, for all that you do as a strong black man. Society has placed a lot of traps for you to fail. Every time our culture, black men specifically, is under attack, our black queens will begin to remind you about your infinite value in hopes of restoring you. You must not slip or lose your grip to your throne, King. When you do, then you will see your own worth diminish. Your freedom is real. Freedom is colorless and rightfully available to all of us. It is not just available to a specific nationality. It is already here within all of us."

Charles stood there in the doorway waiting patiently to leave as he replied, "Thank you. Give me a kiss. Are you ready to head out? I'm starving."

"Yes, we can place the order in the car," Tremaine said.

"Damn, Baby, that's deep. You are absolutely right about what you said earlier."

She continued their conversation as the two of them strapped on their separate seat belts. "Baby, we must re-program our minds to get rid of what we have been taught. Think about it? Every time something monumental happens within our black culture, for example, the evil attempts to persuade us with tainted images or words of our black men as lesser with limited value. Look at how Trump took a shot at Lebron on Twitter! He was insinuating that the brother is dumb. DUMB? For what? Opening an educational institution... the I Promise School?"

Charles continued driving, then placed one hand between his legs. "See, that's facts. Shit, you just made me hard talking to me like that." Charles stopped at the red traffic light on the corner of Marietta St. N.W., near the car wash across from the convenience store and shopping plazas.

"Sweetheart, you have overcome these obstacles. I've watched you turn your nays into yay. There were no seats left; you brought your own, and that's sexy. I just want you to know I am extremely proud of the man you are. I want you," Tremaine said, shaking her head as she looked at the pedestrian walking by on the sidewalk. She realized she was on a tangent running her trap. "I know I went on and on knowing you're hungry, Baby," she openly admitted.

Charles uttered, "Uh huh hungry for you." Tremaine looked around to take advantage of his personal holiday.

Then, she noticed a car wash sign that read: *Pull Into the Wash*. Charles was taking a moment, indulging into all the chocolate in front of him. He kissed Tremaine gently on her neck while the light was still on red. When it changed to green, Tremaine said, "Charles, turn in there."

He reiterated, "In here? The car-wash?"

"Yes, you said you were hungry and felt dirty, so let's get a quick wash before you eat." Tremaine paused to glance at the carwash options. "Choose the deluxe wash, because you deserve the works," she said.

As he threw the change into the machine and pulled in and parked, he spoke calmly. "Cool."

Streams of soapy bubbles and water splashed against the windshield and poured continuously as it changed colors from blue to orange and yellow, alongside the car. The automatic car wash was the perfect hideaway. Tremaine catered to him within the time allotted for the wash.

"You are so spontaneous," he whispered.

"What is more powerful than you, my king?" she replied.

"Not a DAMN thing!"

"Uh huh, and I know you like it like that."

He moaned from satisfaction.

"Each time I hear your voice...
I breathe again;
Baby, it's surreal
Each time I imagine your touch...
I pant for more of you
In my dreams...
If not nothing else
I would just rather die..."

Epiphany: Longing for Sandcastles

Well, who would have thought a small town, southern girl would have the answer to discovering life's treasures? Words assembled into sentences forming planned ideas of meaningful objects or ideas. We choose not to ignore the unappealing moments of idiotic stupidity at its finest.

The uncanny notions of wasted words slammed together to distract pure magical discoveries merely. There are many reasons behind the making of shaky structures. It starts with poor planning and cohesiveness, as well as, poor quality of materials used to hold things together. The proper reassurance into finding innovative ways of making sure our most valuable belongings are kept intact.

Nowadays, most structures are not built upon a solid foundation. At times, other structures are built upon shaky foundations that aren't built to stand the test of time. These innovative ways can stimulate desires to acquire new skills, additional support, including the adequate time to allow evidence of steady growth, built upon solid, resilient foundations to come.

Fantasy

Deep sleep lurked over my body
To my surprise, a chocolate delight
Which seemed to appear as tall & handsome
To my eyesight;
With red stem roses in a bundle
Dark brown skin
And distinct black eyes
Which made my heart crumble;
He appeared so well-groomed
Until I just assumed
Truly he was heaven-sent
Which forced me to want to tamper with time
And treasure every moment spent;
Skin as smooth as honey
Smile bright and sunny
He placed me in his arms
We reached a calm and safe place
To guard and protect me from harm
In his hand he held a sparkling
Diamond;
His manly voice uttered, "Will you...
I quickly uttered, "YES!"
What is coming over me?
It was just another ... darn
Fantasy...

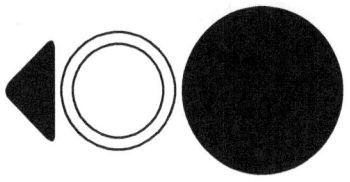

CHLOE

Chloe didn't know what her dreams meant at the time. She didn't know how to interpret them. The dreams appeared strange. She just knew everyone was panicking, running as usual. This time, the sprint was dark and life threatening. It wasn't the ideal competitive match that they were accustomed to. It was mostly her track teammates who were running for their lives through the woods in the neighborhood; and then, Chloe woke up from the nightmare.

Dr. Olay asked, "So, at that time, Chloe, you must have been hysterical?" Chloe attempted to respond while sweating underneath her armpits.

"Yes. Then again, for no reason; it led up to our last practice of our upcoming spring break. The coach told us to be safe during the break. We didn't go into specifics on ways to keep safe. There was this huge spring break party at the local spot and everyone who was somebody was in attendance. Malcolm and I had a very close bond together. We were both in the school's track club, and I can recall, plenty of times, I would join him to practice racing with his male counterparts on the team. Collectively, I would out race some of them and they thought it was the coolest thing ever. Of course, they didn't want anyone to broadcast around the school that a chick beat them in a race. I made it my business to never let them forget it whenever we were together."

"Did Malcolm have reservations about your defeat against his team mates?"

"No, although, he knew it was a sensitive topic for some reason. Malcolm and I were childhood neighbors. Malcolm, his step sister, Charlene, and I attended the spring break party. It was held at an old neighborhood community building mostly used for meetings or private functions. I never realized the place only had one entrance and exit door. Honestly, it was a tragedy waiting to happen. As a teenager, no one is interested in how many entrances and exits are available. The party was lit and overcrowded; and we pretty much saw most of our high school track team in there. We were having a blast, too. I mean everybody seemed to be having so much fun. Malcom and I were dancing in the middle of the dance floor, along with Charlene.

Until..." Chloe's heart paced faster as she felt an urge to continuously perspire underneath her armpit, and her skin crawled as she attempted to maintain her composure.

Dr. Olay asked, "Chloe? Chloe? Until what?"

Well, there went Chloe's cool, out the window. As her left hand moved uncontrollably, she started shivering and her stomach churned. Chloe placed her right hand over it to try and diffuse the movement. Meanwhile, her head was nodding in a *no* gesture as Chloe was trying to avoid this memory within the tragedy. She stalled for time to gather her thoughts together. As she glanced at the clock to see if maybe their session was almost over, she asked, "What was that, Doctor? Olay?"

"You were saying everyone was having a blast, including you, until what took place, Chloe?"

Chloe's nervousness was getting the best of her. She continued, "Until we heard gunshots on the outside over the loud music from the deejay booth. The music stopped as time stood still in the dark where everyone stopped dancing, then the lights came on. Charlene started to scream hysterically next to me, 'NOO!' Then, I began hyperventilating, with dry mouth and chills, because we both realized our dancing partner, Malcolm, wasn't standing beside us. He was slumped over on the floor in a puddle of blood near the side of his face. It appeared Malcolm was dead from a gunshot wound, with his brains exposed from his right side above the eye. Charlene and I both had remains of Malcolm's flesh and blood on our clothes. The bullet could have been for either one of us. Minutes later, Malcolm's killer walked in through the only door to escape in the entire building, holding a firearm in his hand. He looked down at Malcolm's corpse, then stared directly at me. I felt my chest and windpipe close. He, then, raised the deadly weapon up straight in the air, rounding off more clips of bullets into the ceiling. Every single person scattered like ants in one great room with very limited space to take cover. I went into a complete glare on the wall, while faintly saying, 'They counted me out; excluded me.' Still, God stepped in and placed his angels all around us to shield us from evil."

Dr. Olay interjected, and posed the question, "Why do you say they counted you out, Chloe? I mean, you are living and breathing to talk about it; yet, unfortunately, Malcolm isn't."

Chloe answered, "The news spread quickly of the ordeal. My family and close friends were told it was either Charlene or myself who was shot in cold blood."

Dr. Olay interrupted again, "Wait, what happened to Malcolm's killer? Did he continue his killing spree?"

"God granted us grace, because he stepped in and calmed the storm. Short term, the murderer took a few steps inside, shooting in the ceiling. Then, he turned around and proceeded outside of the building. Long term, he is currently still serving a life sentence for the murder of dear Malcolm to date."

Epiphany: Iced Pumped Hearts!

Even the high temperatures don't melt all the ice hearts in the summer. We are in for a challenge to survive amongst the cutthroat souls that lurk on the innocent just to get recognition. There must be a process of marking the cold from the warm at heart. We should exercise categorizing everyone inside our daily circle, whether it is at work, church, school, or even at home. Then, we will come closer to controlling the mediocre in our radar and circumvent any foolery aimed at distracting us from our goal.

They prey on the innocence by upstaging a selfish gain of money, power, and respect. Our stolen choices are stripped from our souls and anchored in their shameless pool of low self-esteem, unhappiness, and envy. Nevertheless, we must remember that everyone is granted a choice in every decision presented, yet, thieves have acquired a skill of raping victims of their earned choices.

We must learn to equip ourselves with the knowledge to take back our choices that lead to taking back our lives. Practice what you preach, walk it like you talk it, be a model of the exact desire you have towards attitude, discipline, work ethic, and character. Allow them to see firsthand what it's like from start to finish. Sometimes, we need to do something tangible to move us from dark times in the direction of our dreams.

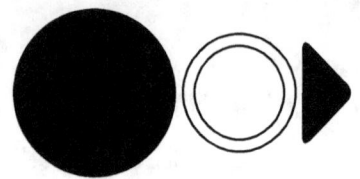

DR. ANASTASIA OLAY

"Chloe, you have cracked the code. You are on your pathway to recovery. I want you to realize that early trauma is a main sign and ultimate representative of neurotic-spectrum problems and physiological health outcomes. These problems can appear as anxiety, sadness, and relationship issues."

"So, this is the reason I'm still living single, huh?" Chloe asked.

Dr. Olay replied, "Yes, it is highly imperative that you understand this underlying past trauma triggered other minor issues within your future to cause road blocks from your ever-deserving happiness. We have reached a visible point of discovery by revealing what caused your fear back then in your adolescence. Although, the true victory lies in discovering what causes your fear, in the now, it is your true avoidance. My whole objective is to help you feel and manage better now. It could be you may have grown strong feelings for Malcolm, and with the tragedy of his death, it allows you to think that when you are interested in someone, you totally lose them...literally."

Chloe proceeded to give feedback, as if she had a revelation. "You know, Doc, I never considered that, because we never admitted to liking each other. We were just great friends. I will agree, Malcolm definitely had a special place in my heart."

"You see, Chloe, even with experiencing trauma, most people are resilient, especially with the condition. There are positive, active, social relationships present in their lives. There are highly skilled, mentally-ill, psychological practitioners who use trauma tactics as a form of treatment to manipulate their patient into performing diversified acts. It is the reason for some tragedies in our society, such as, bombings or armed shootings in schools, churches, and public places to accomplish their own political agendas, like 9/11 and the World Trade Center, for example. All I am trying to say is, you have the capability to survive, recover, and adapt to healing your life to be free from this trauma, to live a balanced life of peace, love and harmony. I feel this will be our very last session, because we have discovered you are truly capable of overcoming this effectively. The source of your trauma stems from your childhood, which rippled outwards into your adult life. Luckily, you were wise and steadfast with avoiding other means of coping with the tragedy by avoiding mental health challenges, alcohol, or drug addictions. You sought out therapy and you held on to it as your life depended on it."

Chloe stated, "Well, it actually did, up until this moment. I always wondered why other track members and classmates who were there that night didn't have the struggles that I have, dealing with it internally."

"Chloe, you never know. They probably have been struggling, also, through different outputs such as alcohol, violence, or bad marital affairs, abuse, flirty, promiscuous behavior... everyone copes differently. Hopefully, you have assurance in trusting our therapeutic treatment methods. I believe by you processing the pain and acknowledging the trauma, it stirs you into your safety and stability, and is the goal to ensuring your path to success. I want you to participate in yoga; and any meditation therapy, such as focus groups, dancing, or fitness classes, stimulates releasing the negative energy that lingers in your body after childhood trauma.

As part of your treatment plan, I want you to slow down and enjoy the finer things life must offer. This effort will guarantee that you take a deep breath and rest easy by practicing mindful acts of kindness. By doing so, it will automatically create a healthier atmosphere by decluttering your current environment. You can slowly detach yourself from technology to provide your internal clock with a reset, assuming you will. There is so much hidden propaganda and secret agendas that society has on this world in the physical realm, including virtually. On the assumption, you take the time out to laugh, even at yourself, while enjoying your time with the people who mean the most to you-your family and friends. Always remember, they are in your corner; lean on them for support. Lastly, I want you to begin a journal to write down your thoughts on a piece of paper, and by the end of the year, I want you to just set it on fire as an act of moving on without it. There's nothing like writing out your thoughts and feelings to release any doubts and depressive emotions you are experiencing. Now is the time to implement a better, healthier you by engaging in physical activity and better eating habits; by golly, pick up a good book. Spruce up your love life."

"Ha! Funny. What love life?" Chloe asked.

"If you haven't found it just yet, visit Jamaica. Go get your groove on. You'll find it there. In this case, recharge your love life; it's still alive!"

"So, is there a particular order to when to start or prioritize these things?"

Dr. Olay replied, "Chloe, honestly, there's no right way to work through your trauma; only ways that make sense to you, and ways that don't. I need you to tell yourself 'this is what I want for myself,' whether that be a man, a house, and a carriage. In other words, you can have anything you desire."

"I think I get it, Doctor Olay. Thank you for all that you have done for me. I will always remember you for giving me the keys to my happiness again."

Dr. Olay turned to Chloe and smiled, "You had it all along, Chloe. I just had to clear off the pathway so you could reach down and pick them back up, darling. Please keep in touch with me. I want to hear about your success stories."

As Dr. Olay watched Ms. Chloe Fields leave the office for the last time, ready for what was on the opposite side of that double door, she placed her right hand over her heart and murmured, "Good luck to you."

As Chloe exited Dr. Olay's office, she received a text message from Travis. It read....

Late night workout session in 3 hours. Would love to see you there at the gym.

Chloe immediately replied...

Okay, see you then ...with joy.

Unforgettable

Nervous at first, that I was
Afraid to open up
And give my love
To you I knew the night would never end
Taking a chance at love had fulfilled a passion deep within
Feeling and holding you
Grasping for more
Time is so valuable
There's so much more to explore
Oh, how much I love thee
Let me count the reasons why
Why I ... I would give my all and
Us a try
Sometimes I portray a
Selfish display
When there's love like this
I don't want to let go
I want it my way or no way
It won't work out
Because if you give your all
then without a doubt
it will last for you and I
We will reach the zenith point by
and by

*Our love will endure crystal clear
Through the years... our profound
Love will mature
Into something very incredible
Then I'll make each night for your
Unforgettable*

Epiphany:
Consciously Intoxicating

There is a rare cluster of individuals who possess an aura about themselves that keeps you engaged in the creativity and newness of endless possibilities. Now, whether the opportunities are self-empowering or downright uplifting to anyone witnessing the magic unfolding before their very eyes.

It is, in fact, hypnotizing to the psyche because of the ability to push any bystander into their greatness. A state, in which, did not occur before the rebirth of visions made every day. It is the true conceptual materializing into the realness of actual accounts of abundant accomplishments. Some witnesses may refer to these encounters as luck, blessings, or favor. The end results are humbled reflections of reflecting on the small beginnings.

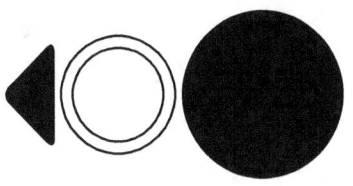

SIMONE

The feeling of Simone's life standing still gave her anxiety in the unknown. She began to flood thoughts of doubtful questions like, *how did I get into this situation, let alone, for nine and a half years of this repeated cycle?* The illusion was crumbling down and her vulnerability was gaining momentum. Simone just hoped the unborn baby didn't inherit any of this torture. She had to do better by being accountable for her own happiness. This was no one's responsibility, just hers.

She looked at all the chocolate melanin that stared back at her in the free-standing, tall Chesapeake, rectangular shaped, walnut, antique floor mirror tucked away in the corner of her rustic inspired themed master bedroom. The focal point in the space was the Chesapeake iron framed California king size bed in the center of the dark wood floors. Right centered above the bed, hung a large canvas of the Chesapeake Bay Bridge skyline wall art. On the nightstand was a vintage round glass of potted orchids.

Holy moly, she never realized how consumed she really was in her marriage. Simone tried to be the stronger one to keep it in the middle of the road. It was time to pullover to the rest area and breathe; and get back to loving herself unconditionally. She had put her all into a man. In a man, who wasn't concerned one bit about her welfare or her unborn child.

Finally, she decided not to keep beating herself up. She tried to channel the reasons why or what other folks expectations were. She was setting the tone and learning how to just say what's on her heart...take it or leave it. Simone was determined to indulge in more passion, and motivational drive to achieve happiness.

Epiphany:
Levels to This!

There are meaningful lessons throughout life to push us in a certain direction. The guided light will progress or regress the experiences we have. Visions can provide answers to partake in the possibilities of our future. We can bask in the glory of the greater in us by seeking it or the opposite, unless we do not wish to acknowledge it.

There are things left in the dark in our minds for which we don't interpret or predict. The unknowing leaves you feeling conquered and defeated. We are just simply not prepared to receive what's in store for us. There are levels of life for which prepare us for the next thing. Should it increase in levels, it only justifies your due diligence is intact. Supposing it is on a declining slope, it is because we have somehow, or some way gone off course and become idle.

Visions of our future are shelved to be picked up at a certain foretold timeframe. Our levels have a real appointed time, whether prepared for it or not. We should dive into our destiny, head first, with arms open wide to receive the many opportunities waiting for us to excel.

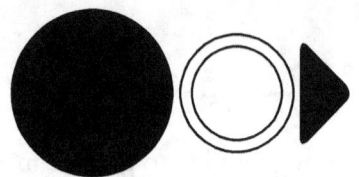

SIMONE

"Ooh, what a kick! There's my little man," Simone said, as she rubbed on her belly, experiencing the baby's movement, as she laid across the bed to really enjoy her son's playfulness across her ribs. "Ouch, now that's rough play. Play fair, Junior." She massaged the area where he was overly aggressive, and prevented him from carrying on. Simone's phone was nearby on the bed so she attempted to take a break from her mind racing. She logged on to Instagram and scrolled down her feeds. *Ugh, so he chooses not to respond to me on his birthday because he's out with the fellas. It seems like a gentlemen's club on 44th street.* Simone was baffled. Thanks, Charles. Obviously, he didn't realize eyes were everywhere with social media as the new wave of communication these days. She realized it was time she started her quest to enjoy life. So, she hit up her girl, Penny, and asked if she wanted to go to check out the scene at Cheeks Lounge on 44th.

Simone facetimed Penny. "Hey, girl, I am craving those hot wings from Cheeks so bad. Let's roll through; its calling my name!"

Penny looked at her through the phone screen with suspicion. "Cheeks? You think they will have drinks specials tonight?" she asked.

"All I know, Penny, is that I must grab some hot wings," she lied.

"Well, you know you can always ask the birthday guy to tag along."

Frustratedly she responded, "Penny, like usual, he isn't here and I choose not to wait any longer to eat."

"Ok, is it okay that I invite Gigi to tag along? We were going to get drinks to catch up?" Penny asked.

"Oh, sure, that's perfectly fine with me. I just need my hot wings and a tall glass of their slap yo mommy Lemonade Tea."

"You are funny. Cool, I'll pick you up in 20 minutes."

"Thanks, friend."

Simone stood up to check out her appearance in the mirror once more. While she tried to figure out how she managed to allow depression to manifest in her life. She pondered ways to combat it, so she uttered, "Yes, it's about time that you begin to know yourself again. I am reintroducing, Mrs. Simone Bison. The beautiful, intelligent, dark-skinned, amazon woman from Madison, Georgia off County Camp Road, to be exact. I will strive to maintain my identity while loving my dark skin." Sometimes there's nothing wrong with meditating, honoring, and praising yourself.

Black Gyrl

Dark as midnight blue
People wondered who
Could be as darker than you
Some mostly ridiculed
In the early stages of life
But now those same people are digging your type
Right?
Tar Baby Black
They called you, while the lighter shades kept things in tact.
Down to the particles of my physique
To the soulful smooth aroma of my feet
Black Girl who's coming to a town near you
Better known as sexy black, dark and lovely, or baby got back.

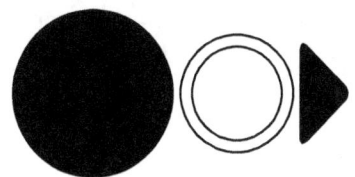

GIGI

When the sun sank, Penelope and Gigi pulled into the Cheeks Lounge parking lot. It was extremely early for the parking lot to be super packed on a Friday night. Cheeks Lounge was an upscale cocktail bar serving alcoholic beverages, and limited appetizers. It's located inside the Midtown area of Atlanta. The new club owners surely were on a mission, indeed, because they knew how to run a successful club. The building was recently remodeled into a trendy, chic, modern *club*. It had a major face lift. As Penelope and Gigi walked into Cheeks Lounge, there was volume from heavy traffic. In the entrance of the lounge, to the right of them, inside the wall fixture, there was a large fish tank filled with colorful, exotic, genetically engineered, fluorescent glow-fish. Colors, such as, electric green, sunburst orange, moonrise pink, star fire red, cosmic blue, and galactic purple vibrant colored tetra tiger barb and sharks filled the tank. The fish tank was one of three of the centerpieces the nightclub highlights as a signature showstopper. The exotic women with exposed cheeks of all nationalities, and the three, nine feet tall stainless-steel vertical stripper poles in the middle of the stage area all set the ambiance. As the DJ spun, the City Girls' remake of the hot track, "I'll Take Your Man," mixed with the original song by Salt 'N Pepa played in the background, setting the mood. The nightclub was setup by all the LED lit cocktail tables. Even the four bar tables were strategically placed around the club and they were waterproof, glowing with LED lights. Those tables were coupled with metal table bases and metal bar stools. It had an eclectic appearance overall.

The bartenders had identical white uniforms which made their outfits glow from the blue hues in the atmosphere, and they were wearing various neon colored necklaces. While they held neon colored martini glasses in their hands, they continuously poured ice and Cheeks Lounge happy sauce into the glasses. The whole lounge was literally lit. The lounge was known for specializing in wings with various flavors.

The inside was super hot, because the crowd was jammed packed. However, the atmosphere and vibes appeared like everyone was having fun as Gigi glanced around the room. She observed Ace of Spades bottles of champagne in the air with sparklers held by the bottle girls, and all the money on the dance floor that led to the VIP section. As a group of clubgoers sang along with the up-tempo version of the Happy Birthday song. Surely it was a pure indicator that the ladies' entertainment is go live tonight.

Epiphany:
Predisposed Booby Traps

Reflections of the past can remove the cover off untold truths. Our focus can be replenished with new inspirations to accelerate the current future within 365 days. This second day of the New Year, we can account for identifying all our real supporters, and, of course, our real haters, too. These facts can lead to great leaps ahead into our positive outlook on Earth.

As we evaluate the traces of our footprints within the past 365 days. We should always know the rightful owner to our future. We should keep an account for the use of our gifts and talents in this jungle of dreams. Indeed, you are the rightful owner of your own destiny, and for that very purpose, to birth your own dreams. You are destined to be good stewards of your very own gifts and talents. In this year's jungle of dreams, make certain to rightfully claim what is yours, and let no man take credit for your fruits and labor.

Our work shall inspire a multitude of dreamers to become inspired to pay it forward. We choose not to look back at our failures. Yet, we will strive to take preventive measures to avoid going under. You have been through hardship before, and you know what it tastes like. You have been through disappointments before, and you know how to assure your satisfaction. You can dispel the make-believe truths, the entire predisposed booby traps, for what they are - a setup for a major come back. We live, and we learn it is an evolving obstacle of experiencing what life has to offer us in this lifetime. There are endless possibilities to explore happy discovery.

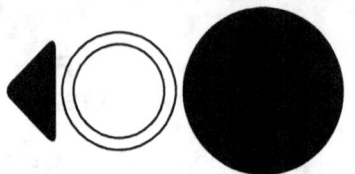

GIGI

As Gigi pushed to the front of the crowd to see where the birthday crew was stationed, across from the bar, she noticed her friend, Katina, in the back of the lounge; and from her view, Katina gave Charles a lap dance while Tremaine sat very close to him. The trio had just made things interesting. Obviously, Gigi didn't get the memo there were going to be fireworks. The décor was very different in their private, secluded section; serving not only liquor and wings, but from her observation, hot ass was on the menu, also.

Really, what was she doing? She seemed to not have enough fabric to cover herself. Gigi said aloud, with a confused look on her face, "I don't remember her telling me she was a stripper."

Penelope looked around the crowd to see if she could spot Simone. "Who?" she asked.

Gigi decided to keep the news under wraps for the time being, while she continued to secretly investigate. "Oh, false alarm. Do you see Simone, yet? I haven't seen her in a couple of weeks or so."

Penelope replied, "I don't see her, yet. Initially, she was supposed to ride with us, then, decided to drive just in case she needed to leave much earlier. Also, so she can find a good table; which was a great idea, considering the crowd. She will be rolling in here in a few minutes ready to eat."

Hearts

Shuffle your cards well
Make your play carefully
Be advised...
Of the deceitful game of hearts...
Where the winner takes all;
Read the rules carefully
To avoid your fall;
Start your play with much wit;
And don't forget
To be aware of the
Game called
Hearts!

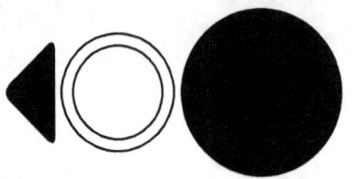

GIGI

Meanwhile, Gigi and Penelope spotted busy body Simone. She was sitting, tucked away in a small table in the cut, excited from observing the various wing flavors on the menu: wasabi, citrus teriyaki rosemary & lime, blackened, famous buffalo, beer battered, chipotle, sesame & almonds, and parmesan. She looked up as they were approaching her cocktail table. "Hi, Gigi, girl! Where did you find Penny Proud?"

Penny laughed as she reached in to hug Simone's large, expanded waistline. "Hi, Mommy Dearest," she said.

Gigi piggybacked off of Simone's inside joke. "Yes, you know that was my show!" Penelope agreed by shaking her head. "Man, those times were the good days. How can you forget about Fat Albert, The Boondocks, and PJs? And, please don't sleep on Avatar the Last Airbender. It's sure to drop nuggets."

As the waiter walked up to their table and took Simone's order, they chuckled in unison.

You are Black As

Black is...
Black as coal on a hot sizzling fire;
Dark as misty clouds;
Black is the color of sleep;
That creeps beneath the eyes;
Black....
Black as night that eventually derives to day;
White is pure;
White is good;
White as snow contrary to black;
Black is the symbolic color worn at funerals;
Darkness is fearful and evil;
Black is blab [gossip]
Black is bizarre
Black is bitchy
Black exemplifies ebonically
Speaking of Black
Black is power
You are black as power!

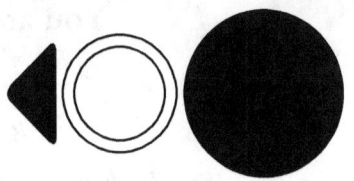

TREMAINE

His happily surprised face was everything Tremaine could imagine it to be in the strip club. Charles was extremely intoxicated. Although, she was a bit taken aback on the fact that he really was very comfortable with this woman. He started rubbing on her nipples and breasts, as if he had touched them before. Meanwhile, this whore was continuously grinding on him in enjoyment. Honestly, Tremaine didn't expect this corner hooker to be there. Literally, the same homeless trick from around the way. She didn't expect her to render the pre-arranged services to him. She really hoped he truly enjoyed his gift, because Tremaine really didn't like this girl. There was something strange about her. She was always popping up when they were together. Tremaine had her antennas up on this bitch for quite some time now. The woman's intuition indicated something was just off.

Now, she witnessed her baby being served a birthday lap dance. Tremaine observed that his "Johnson" was standing at attention, ready. Meanwhile, she was ballistic. Yet, she tried to keep it together like it was a part of her surprise. The truth was, she was on top of him way too long. Tremaine knew she only prepaid for fifteen minutes. Thirty minutes later, things didn't go as planned. *Like, when will she ever go away?* Tremaine thought.

For a second, she thought she overheard grunting from one, or maybe both of them; like they were whimpering with pleasure directly in front of her.

The dancer murmured in Charles' ears, "I really hope you enjoy the rest of your night, handsome. I can do what you like all over again, just for your birthday."

Like hell she will. Tremaine placed her arms in between the two of them and tapped him on his chest. "Oh, it's okay. I can take it from here," she said.

"Chuck likes when I am on top of him," the stripper said, matter-of-factly.

"Excuse me? What did you say? How do you know his name?" Tremaine asked, with an attitude. There went her plans, out the window.

This whore rolled her head, then asked Charles, "Well, do you want me to stop?" And all Tremaine saw was red as she whooped that slut's ass. The nerve of her! Ignoring and disrespecting her like she was invisible.

EPIPHANY: GRANTED GRATITUDE THAT SURPASSES UNINVITING ATTITUDE

Consistent pain overshadows our paths, making misguided decisions in the rut of the hurt and disappointments, both physically and mentally. It is always a challenge watching loved ones or someone you highly respect go through suffering. The helplessness you feel inside, while observing them fight through their struggle. Like, the sense of vulnerability when you walk up to your vehicle and quickly realize you might have locked the keys inside. Or, the nervousness you feel when you've misplaced your cellular phone.

It is very unfortunate to experience for yourself or witness one's struggle at their most vulnerable state. These types of triggers stem several types of attitudes during the disarray. Cling on to thankfulness, forgiveness, love, and hope while finding your pathway.

While everyday may not be peachy, it surely can be covered up in peach scented air freshener. There are so many tragedies everyday of worst-case, real-life situations that can cause the pain to be numb and minute as compared to the neighbor across the street that rarely speaks or maintains their lawn daily.

Once we possess a thankful heart for the few imperfect things, which may depict a perfect picture to someone else in a much worse condition as you, we should appreciate the quality of life we share in this country we live in, when comparing other worldly economic social conditions. America, the land of opportunity, and the land of the free; where we continuously breathe in dreams and birth out visions.

There is a type of pain described as brokenness. The internal massive wound which causes much suffering, yet it can be treated and healed over time with plenty of forgiveness. When we forgive each other of the hurt, it can release tranquility and positive beginnings our way. This type of attitude will grow stronger in time; although, taking the first step in preparedness will lead us closer to our goals.

We all need to maintain or develop a heart that still loves. It can be the remedy to all the pain experienced and encourage mending past connections from hate into love. The spirit of love has a natural ingredient of making all crooked turns straight to ease or eliminate the pain. The hope of a better tomorrow provides a better perspective on things to come.

When we realize we are in control of having the victory to all our undoubted promises. We will visualize our way of life for the better and reverse the misguided paths to bright futures ahead. Once we allow our gratitude to supersede the annoying attitudes, we sometimes possess some, more than others. We can experience all the various layers of accomplishments by continuously reaching our dreams.

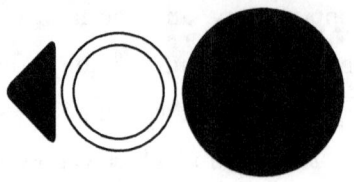

TREMAINE

Ugh, she knew Tremaine didn't like her! She grabbed Tremaine's wig and held on to it tight, as she tried to break free. They continued to squabble, knocking down the Ace bottles and slamming into the glass top on the metal cocktail frame, which startled the clubgoers alongside the private section of the extended VIP area. As Crime Mob's "Knuck if You Buck" played loudly in the foreground, Simone and Penelope approached with some chick Tremaine had never seen before. She cried out to the low life, disrespectful stripper. "Katina!"...followed by Penelope shouting, "Tremaine! Simone, you were dead on, girl! Shit!"

Instantly, the nightclub security grabbed the two of them, in hopes of breaking up the fight and taking control of the atrocious situation. Meanwhile, Charles' trifling ass finally stood up from the table. Then, he had the nerve to acknowledge Simone, then pulled her away to safety, instead of trying to stop the fight. He was very attentive to Simone. Like, he was trying to protect her from getting hit or cut from all the broken glass on the floor.

Simone yelled, "Charles, what is going on? So, now I see why you couldn't come home tonight. You got your hands full. I see you're out here playing a bad hand of Uno, huh?

Puzzled, Charles asked, "Uno?"

Simone replied, "You don't know who you want, so that *Draw 2* ain't work. So, you tried the *Skip* now the *Skip* ain't save you."

Charles responded with embarrassment, "Let's go I'm not sticking around for this mess." Simone started swinging; hitting him on the head a couple of times while screaming, "*Reversing back to me won't save you, either!*"

Charles pulled Simone by the arm and picked her up. He found the emergency exit and stormed out.

Trapped

*Torn in between night and day
the two are so much different
in so many ways;
I am only human
Constantly making mistakes;
To venture out in life
So many choices to contemplate;
Night has always been dear to me
Very supportive and so carefree;
Whom lingers on my every word;
No control no substance, at times
It seems absurd;
You see Night has always had to nurture
The moon and the stars;
While I'm preparing myself
Spiritually;
Night is home with the moon and stars constantly,
Work no play;
Has been my Night's life always;
I'm all Night needs to survive
But, can it be?
Night depends on me to provide her every need;
Night turns into Day...*

Day comes along shining so bright;
Focus and determined to be seen at first sight;
What is that? A rainbow in the sky
Symbolizing every dream
Day wishes to come true;
Day is so intimidating to my intellect;
My Day is so unpredictable
I don't know what to expect;
I'm usually in control
Not knowing what's going to happen
Has me in a standstill
Although I still feel
Intrigued by the way Day
Appears to me;
But you see, I'm all they both got...
I'm their world...Trapped in between, **Night and Day**

Epiphany: Illogical Behavior

Things we do aren't always logical, although they are always doable. There is a behavior we tend to display that will appear to be insane. Others will not understand your actions clearly, or at all. We have been desperately seeking for solutions to constant struggles that occur over our lifetimes, such as pain, unemployment, depression, and legal strife.

As human beings, we tend to build great confidence in people for whatever reasons, and almost every time, these same people will lead to great disappointments. Most of us provide all our mind, energy, and talents to situations or people who aren't even worthy of receipt. We tend to shrink ourselves to fit into circumstances and problems that don't belong to us in the first place. We should practice being more proactive by expanding our territory, instead. There will be a recovery of restoration for our actions.

Our big dreams of success have inadequate space to flourish inside of a mediocre mindset, or one that's filled by other people's problems. There is a constant battle against birthing our dreams. We must always remember, there is a victory in every battle. We will remain focused and faithful that our visions come to pass. There is increase and prosperity just waiting to happen for us. These supernatural increases will allow us to possess territorial dominion over our lives.

These encounters are not by circumstance or not by mere intent. The interactions between any living object or being sparks levels of energy required to pull or push us. How can we afford to be pulled down the wrong path due to inattentive behaviors? We all can benefit from reflections of real, intoxicating encounters of thought provoking occurrences. Then, once we decipher and unlock the underlying message behind it, you will know when it is happening based on the way it made you feel. Will you be too consciously intoxicated to interpret your next move?

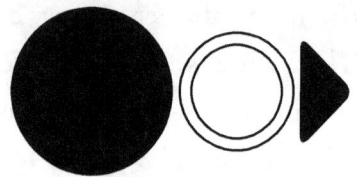

PENELOPE

The next morning, Penelope stood in the break room preparing her normal cup of coffee with six cubes of sugar coupled with creamers. Dreadfully realizing she was at work for eight long hours on a beautiful Saturday morning. There was a major software update of her company's primary desktop application servicing well over ten thousand users. So, the less effort of interruption of work for the majority of the building would happen on a day they are mostly not at work...the weekend. At that instant, she made a promise to herself. She planned to stay busy having fun on her weekends. Immediately, Penelope whispered, "I haven't worked on a Saturday in decades."

Yet, the good thing from these efforts, would be the extra cash in her paycheck for the overtime worked that pay period. The thought of more money boosted her morale as she stood there with a calm grin stamped on her face.

A call came in, and sure enough, it was a collect call from the state of Virginia prison.

"Hello? Hey, how are you?"

Jeff replied, "Baby, it's Saturday. You are supposed to visit today. Where are you?" Penelope answered, "I know, but I am here at work today. We are deploying some important changes. But, we should talk later this evening. I need to tell you about the fiasco that took place last night at Cheeks. Chuck has lost his flipping mind."

Jeff responded, "Cheeks? Well, I know it's crazy you're calling my boy Chuck instead of Charles. I can only imagine what it is about."

"Yes, Cheeks. It's a long story. Simone is expected to have the baby any day, and she was craving their wings; and he is being unfaithful, as expected."

Jeff asked, "Hold up, how is that expected, Penny? You expected that didn't you?"

Penelope replied, "No, I didn't expect it; Simone did. Despite her warning to me, I felt like she was being overly cautious. However, I didn't know why? Because, she had a hunch something wasn't right."

Jeff interrupted, "Oh, there y'all go with your woman's intuition crap."

"Right. A woman's intuition will get you every time. I feel terrible, too, because I defended him when she had insinuated earlier this month."

"She doesn't need to be stressed, because they're baby will feel it, too."

"Exactly. It was just so embarrassing for her and the two side pieces involved," Penelope said.

Penelope heard someone approaching the area. She decided to do a whole bunch of explaining later tonight when he called back, because Penelope quickly hung up, as opposed to getting fired for being caught on the phone.

3D Glasses

My heart just hit the bottomless floor
The outpour of pure sweat and tears not to
Mention sweet caresses and love has been shoved out
That damn door
Did you think I wouldn't think to ask?
What I've grown to know
Did you think I would allow you to run the show completely?
Even without pouring me
The same measurement of value
That I've already poured into you
Or even have you attempted to come close to
Each time you kiss her
I can taste the bitterness
Each time you throttle her
I lose my air fighting for my next breath
I guess you really didn't realize
What you should've already come to know
Well, baby let me tell you
I am fully aware of my outpour and illuminating glow
This light in me came on for you
when our very souls connected as one
each encounter was pure truth
Baby don't dim the lights down low
Don't be afraid to cut the light off

Just let the whole thing go
Because seeing is all knowing
Yet it's like you're wearing a pair of 3D glasses
To see the bells and whistles at its best
You must already have them on
Obviously, you left your 3D glasses behind
This time...

Epiphany: Flawless Errors!

Many times, we are exposed to all the things we have done wrong, first, before acknowledging anything we have done right. Human repertoire of multiple mistakes happens continuously. Yet, it should not define our essence as a people. It is in our psyche to remember what our failures are before basking in the glorious victories. As a child, we were taught to sit up straight, to speak proper English, and to say Amen at the end of our prayers.

All the traditions and rituals can manipulate our true way of thinking; altering our voices over the years, losing our identity due to hiding behind traditions that were mostly *set up* through stories or in school history books. Those before us made the same mistakes, too, and that cycle continues. Their hidden flaws still show a pillar of respect to their power or image. As we enter 2020, let us refrain from seeing our wrongdoing and practice uplifting the beauty in human lives. This energy will spread to generations and future generations to come. Cheers to a better you! Hello, 2020!

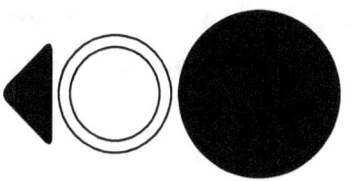

PENELOPE

Rasputia walked up to greet Penelope. "Good morning, Penelope," she said.

Penelope replied, "Hello."

She continued in a direct tone. "What is the status on the report conversion project?"

"So far, there is a hold waiting on the updated procedures to be approved in development," she candidly replied.

"Well, that shouldn't take too long to receive feedback. I want to have it in my inbox by close of business Monday. By the way, I heard you had a nice bump in pay when you came over to the division. Must be nice."

Penelope interjected, "Surely, not in the proximity of your pay."

"You should come and hangout with us this evening," Rasputia persuaded.

"Oh, I have plans to take my dog to the park later. He has been at home all this week alone. So, I must show some love to him today, for real. Thanks for the invite, though," Penelope replied.

As Rasputia walked off without blinking, she stretched her eyes with a stiff smirk on her face like The Joker. Penelope felt the heat from Rasputia's blood boiling from anger. Clearly this black woman has an identity problem. Penelope read her face based on her expressions. Her wrinkled forehead revealed she contemplated and researched her approach with Penelope today. It was a true indicator of her selfishness and cold lack of empathy for anyone.

When Penelope's Aunt Betsey was still living, she was very good at judging someone's character by their face or body language. She imagined Aunt Betsey now, saying, "I don't know, Penny, her forehead is too slanted back. She is a straight criminal!" Oh, Penelope pictured her pointing out that long index finger in the air talking about, "She is a thug."

Penelope was unsure as to why Rasputia was targeting her. She saw the signs from the very first day walking into this place. So, why should she play along? For what? To act naïve as to what was happening now? Seriously, She didn't have time for it. Penelope expected the chips to fall as they may and the explosives to be devastating in a few days. It wouldn't surprise her. She was prepared for a World War Z episode starring her very own race of people, and gender at that. Typical.

Envy don't hate me

Don't hate me because I'm loved by many
Don't hate me because I treasure every penny;
To be able to receive everything
My heart's desire;
Don't hate me don't get worked up to perspire
Don't hate me because I have goals
While you are out hating, digging
Yourself in a deep hole
You see, What God has for me
It is for me
Your hating in the world
Will bring shorter days in your lifespan
Don't hate me because
I possess the masterplan
Don't hate me
Hate yourself
For not being loved by many
For not saving every penny
For not having goals
Digging yourself in a hole
An early grave
Don't hate me
Because I'm blessed
Spiritually

What God has for me
It is for me
God knows what's best
And you don't
Only God can judge me, while He's watching you

EPIPHANY: SCORCHED OPPONENTS

How can the whole world be truly happy when the next person is feeling agony? How can we refrain from sharing the outpouring of knowledge when there are starving ears? Assuming only that there were a collection of equitable love for all mankind, where there is no fear of competition. A new day approaches when Felipe provides a word of encouragement to Hakeem prior to taking their final chemistry exam. Or the track coach credits her sprinter's effort even after Felicia's unsuccessful quest of breaking the high school 400-meter dash invitation meet. Wins can all be redefined by how we internalize the real initial reasons.

We can all become leaders. True heroes in our local neighborhood canvassing ongoing support of helping others visualize the same. Let's not dare to forget the individuals assigned to supervise other human beings at the workplace. They should be, and remain encouraged to share consistent knowledge. The simple fact is management holds the key to influencing death and life into employees. There is a very tactful sensitive skill to assigning the right person to manage groups of people. Past and future reflections will caramelize into a beacon of light in others' darkness.

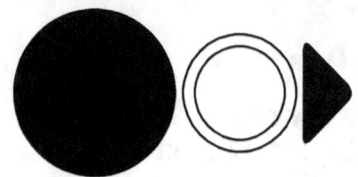

PENELOPE

Sometimes, Penelope always wondered why people felt intimidated by her presence and inner being? She seemed to think she was a normal, loving person who would give her last to someone in need. It never failed, even Penelope's own family members had personal issues concerning her, and she wholeheartedly believe she was innocent in the whole assumption. Penelope was convinced there lies a small, transparent cloud of favor over her life. She believed she should always carry herself with class and dignity and have forgiveness in her heart for others' actions. It was in our human nature to have hate for the fellow man or woman at free will. It was something passed down to us in our culture and upbringing, unintentionally or intentionally. A woman's purpose in life is to continue to receive, create, express and nurture. Yet, as a man, they were taught at an early age to be domineering. Staying busy, and doing something to juggle multiple things demonstrates power and importance. If there was anything outside of those means, then the men were considered a failure. Their value of life was determined by money. Having the right career, or car granted access to their self-worth. Because, our society often reminds our men that they are not allowed to show any signs of weakness. What does a champion look like? They are approachable, caring, loving, trustworthy, respected, transparent, inspiring, resilient, enthusiastic, praised, and recognized.

Penelope sat at her cubicle desk compiling all the testing results from their black box testing for documentation. She sat reflecting how it was overdue to perform her daily affirmation exercise.

Inside the African American social environment, law enforcement fears our black skin. Our reality is, being caught driving, walking, or at home while black weighs heavy on our very own existence as a people. In other words, land of the free that society has built around us, it is not truly free for all mankind. There are a select few in the world who are setup to be free in this conditioned environment.

Until now, the media and local and federal officials distracted the reality of our condition by entertaining spoofs, such as the illegal coaching allegations yielding Naomi Osaka in defeating Serena Williams.

While black men like Botham Jean and Trayvon Martin's lives ended through gun violence and police brutality in the corrupted race relations in our nation. Increasingly, while we plea to political officials to develop more gun reform. Religiously, Penelope tried to show more love through positive words exuberating more light in a dark world, especially in a world of evil and heartache.

Maybe she should encourage herself routinely, because she trusted God. She knew He has great plans for her. Penelope would acquire great accomplishments because of her obedience to listen and adhere to godly advice from godsent people. While she, at least, attempted to do mostly everything according to God's will, yet, she acknowledged she was not perfect by a long shot. On the other hand, she knew surely He would keep His word; and it was enough for her to prepare her future on this day. Penelope's affirmation was just to continue to speak life into her life, in Jesus' name.

She had the power to flex her muscle of influence by understanding the pure difference between going to school, being educated, and now, possessing knowledge. Penelope's mind was iron sharp after realizing she is much more clever, robust, and better-off at being serene with things in her exterior.

Penelope's coworker, Peter, who sat across from her cubicle ducked around the short partition wall separating their working spaces. "We have one more hour to wait," he whispered with content, as their freedom drew near.

This was all a monopoly game inside of a transparent bubble. Every human being is live, in living color, inside of a preconditioned *setup*. The only way to obtain the wealth of success is to become more human to overcome all evil.

Penelope was willing to be responsible for empowering others and willingly share her influence and position with others. She will begin by delegating her authority by empowering other human beings to take initiative by investing in other people's dreams. She knew by starting that day, delegating small tasks to others, she hoped to someday empower.

Penelope gazed at the computer screen thinking, *Tremaine, you should feel dirty. I mean low down dirty.* So, she sent her a text.

How long have you been messing around with Chuck? Right underneath your friend, your sister, your ace boon coon. Once upon a time, I thought you two were closer than I was to you. The weird part about it, I feel like I have some part in it. I should have seen the clues or some type of sign that you and Simone's husband had something going on! For goodness sake, the woman is pregnant with his baby, T! Does any of this mean anything to you? You are so ruthless and cold. You just remember on this day what I told you, because you best believe what goes around comes right on around, and I am all here for it.

Burglar

Loved by many
Despised by most creed
Accused of taking advantage
Of other's needs;
Due to a lack of security
They see;
Or perceive me to be
Some...burglar
That takes and takes and
Then tries to create
A bond between the two
So that you won't have
A clue

EPIPHANY: RAVENOUS VISIONS!

Visions are mental "selfies" of desirable actions over time. The enlightened possibilities shed, foretell sunshine vividly into our future. There are key lessons intertwined in revealing our road map to success.

First thing's first, we must capture the idea in hindsight to reflect and allow it to materialize by writing it down. Secondly, reality will set in while we are taking these ideas into consideration. The steps of envisioning where we are headed sends tranquility to our inner soul.

Thirdly, affirmations will strengthen our beliefs in attaining these visions. Subconsciously, we will begin to accelerate and achieve the written things, better known as goals. Melodic voices will develop; internally persuading us to grab hold to our visions and don't let go. We must continue to possess a ravenous appetite into achieving our goals.

Sharing authority to the ones you empower by allowing them to make decisions and initiate actions also solves problems publicly. It shows confidence to let them know you believe that they will succeed. Then, it will release them so they are able to succeed on their very own, giving them space to allow them to describe their dream job.

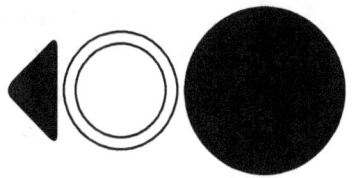

DR. ANASTASIA OLAY

"You are speaking too fast, Gigi, slow down. Okay, you've been looking for Katina?

"Yes, and she is nowhere to be found?" Gigi replied. "I don't know; I should have given her a ride last night. I honestly think something has happened to her!"

Seconds to Minute

Seconds to minutes strikes vigorously
As time passes on day by day
While the signs of winter vast away;
The grey branches turn dark green;
And the cool clouds allow the sun to beam;
Sounds of nature chirping continuously
Minutes to hours strikes
Vigorously;
The flaming humidity
Have no pity
Hours to days strikes
Vigorously;
As day goes by;
Loved ones vanished
As the winter comes around
Time has placed a damper on me
My sight isn't as sharp how it
Used to be
As the days turn to years
Vigorously
While time passes by...
It has flew...
And...
Yet I still...

Long to receive...
A word...
From You...
As seconds turn into minutes and minutes turn...
Eventually to days

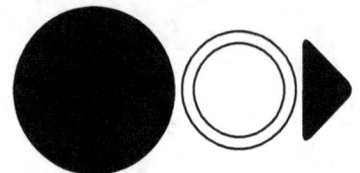

DR. ANASTASIA OLAY

"Ok, Gigi, first come in and have a seat," Anastasia said.

"This is some crazy shit, Stasia. It's like..."

Anastasia interrupted, "Gigi, you act like I was there. What are you really saying? Calm down. Now, start from the top, girl."

"No, I don't want to sit; because, my nerves are too bad right now. Last night, I went to Cheeks with Penelope and Simone."

Gigi stood behind the double glass front door in the Mediterranean entry of the double foyer area of the large atrium. The space had flat white, mixed, thirteen feet ceilings, beige walls, and marble floor. In the middle of the end of the foyer entrance, there was a large bouquet of flowers in a tall porcelain vase. In the open, spacious room, there was a king size chaise and throw blanket laid across the furniture.

"Tasia, my intuition is screaming something just isn't right. Katina was open with me. She told me about being in a long-term, abusive, toxic relationship with a man who gave her a sexually transmitted disease. He would force her to do things unwillingly, such as, pimp her ass out. It's one of many reasons why I wanted you to talk to her."

Anastasia replied, "Talk to her? Talk to her about what exactly because these are bold accusations here, Gigi." In disbelief, Anastasia attempted to maintain her composure. "Yet, you chose to leave that pertinent information out from when you told me about her initially?" she continued.

Gigi agreed, "Shamefully so; because she made me swear I wouldn't say a word to anyone. She was afraid that something was going to happen to her when it leaked out. Lord, I just pray the man she was talking about isn't Charles!"

"What was going to happen, exactly?"

"I mean, I don't know, because I always honored her wishes. It's how I earned her trust. Oh no, what about Simone and the baby? I need to go check on Simone and tell her everything I know. I don't know...I feel responsible for her disappearance."

"Wait, maybe you are overly exaggerating. She could be visiting family, or just plain embarrassed from the situation from last night and just needs her privacy. Let's be rational. Your pregnant friend, Simone, doesn't need any added-on stress from a speculation. Can you describe what she was doing in the nightclub last night, when you saw her there?" Anastasia asked.

Gigi replied, "Funny you asked. Well, technically, not funny. Last night, she was stripping!"

"I am not truly certain when if it's the case for Katina; although, I have been asking you all the preliminary questions I would ask someone who was involved in or a victim of being deceived to do any acts of sexual exploitation, prostitution, forced labor and even slavery or similar practices."

"Tasia, my Lord...Do you think this child was involved in some type of sex sting or human trafficking?" Gigi asked in horror.

Anastasia threw her hands up in the air. "Yes, Gigi, I hate to admit it. You mentioned things that you witnessed yourself. Especially things Katina expressed to you about how she was coerced into doing explicit acts. She was convinced into thinking that if she didn't commit them, some type of threat or harmful force will happen to her. You said yourself, she had several secretive, temporary jobs. Not sure if she was compensated payments or benefits for completing these temporary jobs. I am certain of all the red flags indicating that this young woman was victimized and caught up in human-trafficking." Anastasia dropped her head into her hands in defeat.

"My God, this is right on. Katina was a runaway child caught up in foster care. She was a victim of physical, sexual, drug, and alcohol abuse. She had prior history in the juvenile correctional system, stricken poor, hungry, and homeless. I should have read the writing on the wall a long time ago. She was trying to cry for help to me, Tasia!"

As Gigi bawled in tears, Anastasia reached out to give her a hug to comfort her.

"Gigi, you've done all you could for Katina. How can you continue to beat yourself up, containing all these emotional anxieties? Because, you will get fatigued putting your heart into a cardiac arrest at the rate you're going now. Importantly, you're not a licensed therapist or trained physician in this field. Katina's foster care services were terminated when she became eighteen without proper transitioning survival skills to care for herself. Thank goodness today, there are programs such as, Think of Us, Inc. Hell, you did the right thing by getting me involved."

Gigi coupled herself in Anastasia's arms, tears weeping and falling uncontrollably, as she tilted her head in agreement.

"Maybe, if I was more aware of all of the signs and pleas for help, I could have gotten you involved sooner, and you would have asked those questions much earlier on. Katina wouldn't be missing, because we would have gotten her the help she needed in the first place. I am totally terrified for Simone now more than ever. Unless, what we're describing is the case, then Chuck is a slimy scumbag. Poor Simone, you think you know a person, and they turn out to be the cruelest person in the universe. He certainly is highly capable of anything. I don't trust him. Why Lord? Why did you choose her? She was an innocent young girl. She already had a strike against her when she was rejected by her family. What could make her give her life to someone else so willingly? I just don't understand."

Anastasia responded, "Gigi, we don't know the answers. For all we know this is all speculation and not factual. We must have compassion for all involved and not take matters into our own hands. Because, it can only make things worse. For all we know, Charles could have been caught up over his head into keeping up with a lavish lifestyle or just fell on hard times.

Organ procurement known as organ harvesting, Human trafficking, prostitution, drugs are all lucrative, illegal activities that are done by high profile entertainers, even higher, more powerful authorities, especially in Washington D.C. There is a massive sex trafficking ring happening underground with children and women. They will pay good money to third party, mentally-ill associations to make their dirty work disappear by any means necessary. The #MeToo Movement is making a sounding alarm and making their voices heard clearly. The public is now becoming widely aware of how this is affecting women across this country everyday. We are witnessing our famous entertainers being exposed on television and mass media streams.

Charles could have been a pawn in it all, just looking for a quick come up. Maybe he intended to get involved temporarily, thinking no one would catch him slipping. Then, the unthinkable happened; manifesting like cancer, just spreading rapidly, until one day, it all caught up to him. Katrina was trying to stand up to life's challenges that many of us experience; a simple life just take for granted.

Meanwhile, victims are lying by the roadside robbed and wounded, caught in that fast life. Baby girl, there are so many others All you can do is pray for peace and help other victims caught in underground, sex cult, pedophile rings, such as Pizzagate.

Sex rings are increasing thirty-five percent in one year alone. It is sickening, because organizers have their own, unique language to prostitute children. Orphanage and foster care children are being flown into some of the most powerful places within living quarters as sex slaves. I want you to read a book in your spare time called, 'Why Johnny Can't Come Home.' Afterwards, I want you to watch a movie called, 'The Boys from Brazil.' There's an alarming rate of eighty-three children per hour disappearing.

Now, we have genetically modified foods and human cloning occurring in our era more rapidly. Should you not believe me, then pay closer attention to your surroundings. You should stay in tuned to government policy administration, such as National Human Genome Research Institute."

Gigi asked, "But, what does genetically modified foods and human cloning have to do with us suspecting Katina possibly being involved in traficking?"

Anastasia replied, "As African Americans, we must stay woke and not sleep on these new legislation laws that are being passed, such as, genetically modified foods, including human cloning. The laws are designed to keep the healthy healthier and the rich richer while the poor become sicker. Prime example, cancer, HIV/AIDS, and all these new diseases are designed to wipe us out. We will destroy our own population by trying to keep up with the Jones' or the Kardashians and Carters."

Epiphany:
A Multitude of Refractions in Multiple Distractions

There are many subtle, subliminal distractions that are done without notice. Have you ever noticed when someone yawns, you instantly have the uncontrollable urge to yawn as well? A multitude of refractions can deter you from your goal in positive or negative ways. Should we learn to stay focused and reflect on the things accomplished, it will quickly speed up the process to success. We can all improve our organizational skills, time management, and cheer squad activities to expedite our road to success. This behavior can have a tremendous life-changing impact on our personal and professional lives!

A quick shopping list or written estimate of the monthly bills provides a good outlook on things ahead. Yet, there is always that one obnoxious distraction of unplanned expenses, such as a flat tire, sickness, etc... It usually throws a monkey wrench in things. During the surprises, we can adopt a way of staying calm while embracing the change. A simple to-do list can increase our productivity, and quality of life while maintaining a relaxed state. Planning our day allows us to use our time more wisely. We can include a nice brisk walk or visit to the ice cream parlor before or after handling the unplanned activities. How we spend time on social media outlets can become a distraction from our goals. So, we should always remain conscious of our time.

Personal cheer squads exist all around us, either as positive or negative reinforcement. You will find it beneficial to routinely evaluate the players of your cheer squad for effectiveness. They are designed to keep us on track of the big win. We have distractions within our cheer squad hindering the progress. We simply must pay attention to the cheer squad player. Who on your cheer squad is intentionally or unintentionally a distraction in disguise?

We must remain leery of who we call our cheer squad players. In this world, we share room enough for a multitude of refracted distractions to stir us in our designated temporary or permanent assignment. Once, we possess a multitude of distractions and attain the lessons learned, it will gain us more knowledge to change the direction of our goals. It will allow us to alter the original to do list to maneuver and take a more sensible detour.

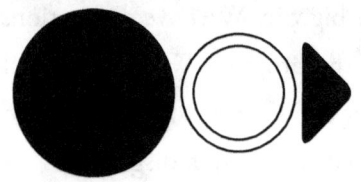

DR. ANASTASIA OLAY

"I'm telling you, in my field, I see the evidence through multiple mind control tactics, such as MK Ultra. It really is a dark world of human exploitation right before our eyes through media, popular music, and videos simply using *trigger words and* secret signage like *butterfly and angel wings symbols,* and code language like, *cheese pizza, hotdog, pasta, ice cream, walnut, map, sauce, automatic, bottom, kiddie stroll, lot lizard, and track,* just to name a few," Anastasia professed. Gigi moved her head in disagreement, "Tasia, you are really freaking me out right now."

Anastasia raised her hand up then dropped it in frustration, "Hell, Gigi, they are even using harmless, cute emojis to sell our babies electronically. We got to be in-tune to catch it, or else we will lose one to the fold. We were off our game, all worried about the Preachers in Hollywood, Bet Awards, Basketball Wives, Housewives franchise or Love & Hip-Hop reality TV shows. They have it all *setup* for whatever you like. It's all a trap for the ones caught off guard. They will take us out of here. There already is illegal, human organ harvesting right underneath our noses.

Like Katina, and so many other victims comply, there is mind control programming at its finest being used. They have been psychologically manipulated into some type of tricked love or loyalty by meeting these certain quotas every night, like anywhere between three hundred to two thousand dollars.

I know it's heart-wrenching, but it's true. I see the statistics are on the rise, especially for people of color. Our brown girls go missing by the droves every hour! Every fifteen minutes, we have a person losing their lives to opioid overdose. They are hooked on painkillers like morphine, fentanyl, hydrocodone, and hydromorphone oxycodone like Percocet and Vicodin. This is another way of manipulating the victims into following orders.

You see, these prey are not aware that opioids are painkillers; then advancing them on to heroin and so on. All these drugs are toxic and potent because it can change your brain into having a higher risk of chronic relapse. They can care less because they are craving the feeling all over again."

Gigi interrupted, "I don't know, maybe we should get the police involved. It's out of my league."

"The law enforcement and people in charge of mandating orders to them are all in on it. Even the medical field prescribes opioids to us. Why? We must be in tune to ask our physicians, 'Why are you prescribing me an opioid? Is this the right medication for me? Is there a possibility that I will get addicted to this medication?' Most importantly, 'Are there any non-opioids that I can take as an alternative?' To a person with a prior drug history who is highly unlikely to answer truthfully to the pre-screening questions before seeing the doctor, it is a dog-eat-dog world. It is *setup* and designed to chew you up and spit you out when you are caught blind sighted.

The crime lords are aware of the ones who are subjected to drugs and prey on their weakness and trick them out for power and influence. The incubator for trafficking is safe houses, homeless shelters, foster care systems, jails, and prisons. There are roughly five hundred youths in the foster care system. Seventy to eighty percent of corrective facilities, such as jails and prisons, were previously associated with the foster care system.

The alarming, large mentally-ill group knows it is a breeding ground for human trafficking. Currently, only roughly ten percent of opioid victims are getting treatment. It is a mega lucrative, cutthroat black circuit done right under all of our noses.

There is no adequate amount of treatment centers, prevention institutions, or even legislative discussions in the political scene to address it. It almost appears that the powers that be are the sponsors of pushing opioids out to the frail, potential victims. They will take us out of here quick! It's no lie; we must stay woke to avoid missing the signs, again."

Gigi threw her hands up as if to surrender. "How do we spot it, Tasia? This is an epidemic; how do we know it's happening? Like what are the signs? What to look for and where? So many people need to be aware of this!"

Anastasia placed both hands behind her neck to massage her neck and shoulders. She closed her eyes for a quick second to gather her thoughts. "First, we must be honest with ourselves about the heinous things happening around us in this world and in our neighborhoods. It's so simple to not think about it; so easy to forget about the problems. I believe there are three groups of people in the world...givers, takers, and counters. As soon as we identify which group we belong to, we can be a more compelling race. The counters are the individuals who conditionally give in exchange for something in return. The group of givers possess extraordinary power to expose corruption, poverty, labor, and sex trafficking... I know you, and I are two givers.

We can empower people to *setup* our lives in a positive way. We must educate our people; within our own household is a good start. We have a right to pursue happiness as humans. All humankind has the right to have a chance to live the American Dream. Yet, happiness must be earned, not given to anyone. Every individual must seek to discover their own joy.

We should support powerful givers, like celebrities who believe in humanitarian acts of kindness such as, Ashton Kutcher. He is a part of a sophisticated entity that developed an application called, Thorn. Law enforcement uses a tool called, Spotlight, sponsored by Senator John McCain and other private sectors, which tracks human trafficking of children."

Gigi stared down at the floor then responded, "I am going to do my part, Anastasia. I just never realized these things are happening right before us every day."

Anastasia admitted, "I know if it weren't for my profession, I would be unaware also; so thank you for desiring to be apart of the solutions. We really need more friends or concerned citizens such as you to do the same"

Please Don't Take My Sunshine Away

Forgive me for what I have done
For you created everyone
I will go and stand in a dark corner
And lock myself away for days
To ask for your forgiveness
If it is the only way
If I can gain your trust again;
And treasure your presence
I will be loyal until the very end
There is nothing to rush
You can take my money
You can take my gold,
But, please don't take the only true love
I have to hold
For I have nothing without my sunshine
It is the only thing that is
Truly mine
Please I ask of you
Don't take my sunshine away, Lord!
For I am lost in a world
Of darkness without it

Amen

Epiphany: Enchanted Noises!

"This is a test!" A familiar announcement, followed by a flamboyant sound interrupts our regular broadcast television and radio services. Emergency alert systems are adaptive warnings in our lives. They can be a nuisance to most and a great tune to a rare group. We are constantly surrounded by various noises. It can be by shattered glass, someone speaking, or the neighborhood dog that alerts us when someone is prowling around nearby.

Our verbal and body language, eye contact, and mind chatter allows us to follow our hearts and learn from our mistakes. We learn to take different approaches to life situations and just breathe and relax a bit.

Love language can express affirmations of emotions. We, as a people, really need love to conquer our goals. It can motivate us into our destiny, whether it's physical touch, quality time, or acts of kindness by gifts. Words can speak life into situations for better or worse. How we communicate through verbal and body language can affect the people in your life.

Now just look into my eyes! Why don't you? It's as simple as triggering a blast of happiness in your messenger's life. Our eyes speak volumes and affirm our intentions by looking into another person's eyes. Our eyes possess the map of our inner selves, and it is highly acceptable to be vulnerable.

Why do we carry on mind chatter during an act of listening? We are conscious listeners when we train our quiet minds to be quiet. So, we can be conscious free listeners. Our mind will become cluttered unless we don't release and experience the peace and beauty of positive noises.

Once we allow ourselves to get familiar and fine tune our own verbal and body languages. We will all become better listeners by making better eye contact and releasing some of the mind clutter. A great listener can truly provide encouragement to others. We must keep a record of the type of noise we create to others. *It is a game changer to bigger collaborations and healthy relationships.*

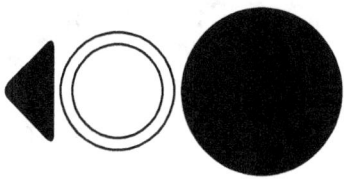

CHLOE

Everything worthwhile takes time.

Travis picked up the chilled bottle of champagne from the marble tabletop. He poured two tall flute glasses of champagne, then proceeded to toast. Chloe lifted her glass in unison.

"Thank you for allowing me a chance to take you out tonight. I'm always grateful to be in your divine presence every chance I get. Cheers to date number ten, and to many more."

Travis reached for her hand to commemorate the moment, then kissed the outer part of Chloe's dark, melanin hand. She naturally blushed, because she couldn't resist the urge.

"That is so sweet. You know that I enjoy being in your presence, as well.

"After sixty days, I think it's time we take this a step up. I feel we have been in this awkward stage of getting to know each other long enough."

Ha! No he didn't go there. He tickled her...and she was all here for it.

If You Wanna Know How I Feel

Like A Princess crowned with a tiara
Like bursting for joy
Knowing you will be there
Like the sexiest woman on earth
Like an astounding, joyous birth
Like an enthusiasm coming over me
Like me and you making history
While we reach our peak
Like spending time during the holidays
Like exchanging gifts
And seeing the surprised expressions on your face
If you wanna know how I feel
Like praising the Lord
With someone real
Like giving you a spare key
To my heart
Like going to the park
Feeding geese with me
Like traveling overseas
But, remember to fasten your seatbelt
While you're in the front seat
Visiting Cancun, Mexico or Greece
So, if you really wanna know how I feel
Be prepared by my response
Because depending on how my day goes
It may be a long one

Destiny and time are on our side
Like helping me cope through sorrows
When a loved one dies
Like reminding me that the sun will shine tomorrow
That's how I feel
Like if you're ready
Be next to the stream while the sunset on top of the hill
I'll be waiting...

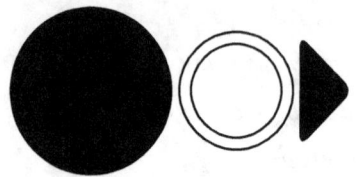

CHLOE

Playfully, Chloe asked, "What do you have in mind?"

Their view on the balcony of the AG Steakhouse restaurant on the second floor, complimented the intensity between them. The two indulged in each other's company, as they sat on the sleek interior leather booth overlooking the electrifying, beautiful night skyline while listening to live jazz. The Ritz Carlton Hotel was a contemporary, fully decorated establishment on Peachtree Street Northeast. The modern, luxury hotel was well known for its southern tradition appeal.

Everything so far had been picture perfect. The food placement on the abstract, square dinner plate was a piece of artwork. Travis ordered for the two of them. For him, an eight-ounce filet mignon, roasted brussels sprouts, coupled with truffle fries. Chloe was surprisingly satisfied with his selection for her... Saint Jacques scallops and grilled asparagus. The five-star cuisine set off sensual flavors of hot, tangy, sweet, and spicy food just the way she liked it.

"I don't want this night to end, so I took the honor of reserving a suite here. In case, we are too intoxicated to drive. Then, I can share all my intimate and most vulnerable secrets with you over a strong nightcap."

He continued to gaze across the table at Chloe. So much, she could sensually feel him undressing her nude, fitted, bandage tube dress. His laser-like, piercing, chestnut brown eyes slowly started to melt away her strapless bra and moist thong by the minute.

"Blame it on the alcohol, shall we?" Travis asked.

Chloe replied, "I couldn't agree more."

Travis flirtatiously responded, "It will be perfect timing, and a prime opportunity to upgrade our situation in the love making department."

Five minutes later, they were passionately displaying their affection to one another by kissing; as he tried to find the button to press while they began making out inside the elevator. Then, Travis started caressing and gnawing on Chloe's nipples uncontrollably, until she whispered, "The elevator is open."

He reached down to grab her long, smooth waxed legs, then lifted her over his broad shoulders as she dangled across his fitted chest. Chloe's head spun from all the rounds of drinks.

As she stared down at his size twelve loafers, she started panting for more of him. The way he walked holding her, was like she didn't weigh one hundred and forty-eight pounds. This moment of pleasure was a clear indication of what was about to go down in the Ritz Hotel, Room 112.

You Make Me Melt

You make me melt like
Sweet molasses showering down from the heavens;
Like the sensual taste of sweet melons
Harvesting in an enrich field
Loaded with lilies and daffodils
You make me melt
And I can't help
This feeling raining down on me
Now, I'm residing in Rome, Paris, Italy
Intuitively speaking of this high
That has me on a rise
Which took me totally by surprise
For I just ... didn't come to realize
After taking off my thick disguise
You make me melt
Like Fire and Ice
Like a caramel Ice cream sundae
With a drop of saccharine honey
Melting inside my heart
Like a bullseye game won
By the cupid's darts
You make me melt like
Perspiration that drops from me
Until it evaporates completely

You make me melt
Yet, you left footprints on my heart
You make me dissolve into you
And it's spectacular
As if you were count Dracula
Are you?

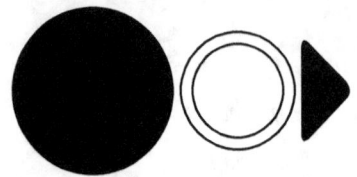

SIMONE

Simone sat in one of the side chairs of the Shorecrest gray bistro table set in the right-angled, secluded, breakfast nook, reading her inspirational novel and reflecting over her life. After the storm settled, Charles and Simone barely spoke to one another, besides conversations about her third trimester and their son's well-being. Simone pondered over what life would be like without Charles in it for their family; because, she put a great deal of unconditional love, blood sweat, and tears into their blessed union. Yet, she reflected on banking on the wrong person as her husband.

Why would he forfeit on their marital investment? Realistically, it was not in far reach to imagine a life excluding him. Would she have enough of a support system raising her child alone? Can she support the two of them financially on her own? Simone predicted seeing her unborn son, along with Charles co-parenting primarily. Yes, an eerie cloud of doubt invaded their fairy tale story, ending in failure. There's nothing left, except to assess the damage while Simone and Charles continually addressed the public embarrassment to all affected, and to all who directly or indirectly influenced their commitment together, emotionally, and financially.

Speechless

Speechless from the pain I feel inside
Disappointed in our results
As the tears hang slightly from my eyes
Speechless of the outcome of our relationship
Hurt by the pain
Speechless now, too much has been said
To patch things up and see what's ahead for us
We've cursed, disrespected one another; stop
Nevertheless, once upon a time I know our love was priceless
Yet, it's shown its true value a long time ago
And that's why I'm speechless.

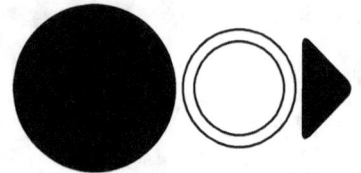

SIMONE

The last couple of weeks had indeed taken its toll on the household. There laid a constant desire to build enough resilient faith in God and self to want better for her and here child.

Simone overheard the garage door open. Charles walked in.

"Hey, how are you doing?" she heard him say. She moved her head all around to make sure he wasn't on the phone or speaking directly to her. Surprisingly, he was.

"Hey, we are doing alright. How was your day?"

Charles leaned in to kiss Simone on her forehead, then sat beside her.

"It was productive. The potential investors seemed impressed with the final investor prospectus, like you suggested. We acquired two new investors to venture capital. Thank you."

Simone replied, "You're welcome. Your business has been taking off for over five years. Good for you."

"Look, Simone, most of the time, I may not have been the best husband. I was caught up and distracted. I will apologize as many times as I must. I promise to make it up to you. I will do whatever it takes to make things better between us. As they say, behind every successful man is a strong woman. I know what you are to me. You have built me up and have been right by my side through the good and the bad."

The doorbell sounded, then Simone asked, "Do you mind if we talk about this later? I'm expecting Gigi and Penny. We're going shopping."

Chuck stood up instantly. "I'll get the door." Then, she proceeded to stand in the pathway. "No, it's ok, I'll grab it." He had really changed into a different person since the drama. And, since the last pregnancy checkup revealed a slight scare. Simone was spotting in her urine prematurely. The doctor ordered her to try and relax more. Hopefully, a shopping trip would be a good downtime for her, as usual.

Epiphany: Traumatic Truths

The notion of truth setting a person free is quite the contrary. Let's talk about when reality caused the cat to escape the bag and leap for the exit. There are dark secrets within most hidden truths, such as personal, family, and just plain out horrible rumors.

Have you ever met a person in yesteryear that personified a different life, and then, witness them change like a chameleon before your very eyes? As people, we live our lives vicariously through others or fantasize about multiple unknown scenarios. The plainest solutions are in staying true within you; allowing things to travel gracefully. Our composure allows inner peace and tranquility into accepting the challenges ahead of where we are going.

There are dark, deep mysteries within every family, painfully hidden. Supposedly, it is for the best interest of family togetherness, when it is the very reason for justifying untruths or unexplained situations. Or, it is merely convenient for the responsible family member to not reveal the truth.

The infamous hearsay floating around regarding negative slander and zero to minimum clues involve the truth. Traumatic experiences create two results, hidden truths or resilient evidence of how to cope with life challenges.

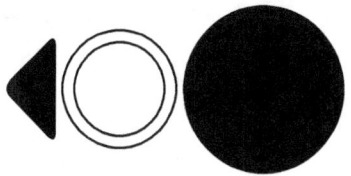

GIGI

"Thanks for deciding to come along and visit Simone to check on her with me. She should be expecting us at 1:30," Gigi said to Penelope, as she pulled up into the circular driveway, then parked her silver Ford 150 extended cab, heavy-duty, pickup truck inside one of the guest parking spaces.

Penelope and Gigi walked towards the walkway to the porch and rang the doorbell. *Ding-dong*, chimed the circular designed smart doorbell camera. "I haven't spoken to or seen Simone in the past two weeks. I am eager about getting her out of this house," Gigi said.

Penelope was rocking from side to side from the anticipation of seeing Simone. "We should go the extra mile to make sure she enjoys herself. At any rate, it should be fun. The flyer stated there will be gourmet appetizers and loads of mimosas and cocktails while shopping at the charity pop-up shop event."

The red double French door with the large, cream, artificial berry grapevine wreath opened. Simone was dressed in a flowing yellow, off the shoulder, chiffon, half sleeve, maxi dress, appearing radiantly beautiful.

"Simone, you look stunning," Gigi said while signaling her hand for permission to rub Simone's large, round tummy.

"Hey, ladies! Thank you. Yes!" Simone closed her door and Penny wrapped her arm around her as they walked back to the truck. Penelope loudly confessed, "I have missed talking to you, girl. Watch your step getting into this monster jam truck".

Gigi entered Interstate 20 East then headed towards East Atlanta Village. She initiated getting rid of the awkwardness by asking the hundred-dollar question. "How have you and the baby been lately?"

Penny chimed in, "Yes, because we have been worried sick about you. Yet, we wanted to respect your privacy."

Simone replied, "Aha, I know you guys mean well. There's no question we have been through it and still ongoing now. At our last checkup this week, the doctor ordered that I relax, because my baby boy was distressed."

"Oh wow, you're having a boy?" Gigi asked.

"Yes. Charles and I have been in a better place for the betterment of our son. I am a lot stronger; just getting to know more about myself while reassessing my emotional and psychological needs throughout this phase in my life, you know?"

"You have arrived," the GPS declared. Gigi scrambled to find a good park, so Simone didn't need to walk as far.

"What phase are you speaking about exactly? Trust me, I had no idea that Katina even knew Chuck. She never gave me any indication she was seeing your husband. Because, you know, I would have been singing like a canary. Well, no offense," Gigi said, referencing the bright yellow, flowing maxi dress Simone was wearing.

"No, none taken," Simone said.

The charity pop up shop event was to benefit a human trafficking prevention initiative. There were several diverse vendors in attendance selling hair extensions, shoes, clothes, accessories, soap and oil. Penelope looked Simone directly in her eyes to say, "I swear on my Fifi." Fifi was Penelope's new charming, one-month-old Pomeranian puppy. "I didn't have a clue that our girl would stoop so low underneath your nose like that. I mean, she is a player by nature. So, I didn't imagine her to have the time or desire to stab you in the back."

Simone placed her right hand on top of Penelope's left shoulder. "How is Fifi?" she asked.

Penelope replied, "She's bad as ever. That's my baby."

Simone picked up a beautiful, pecan tan dress to show Gigi. "This is a nice color on you, Gigi. I have done some soul searching, now I'm just trying to determine if I even want to stay in this relationship. I have been really seeking answers from God to the question, 'what is purposely yours?' You know, as a little girl, I imagined how I would be as an adult, and I imagined the type of profession I would have when I grow up. I was clumsy."

Penelope also confessed, "Yes, I can remember the time you were riding on your ten-speed bicycle, cruising down the hill with your cousin."

Simone answered, "Aha, Elvera. Well, at the bottom of the hill, a silver medium-sized cat dashed out right in front of us. There was no time to brake, only enough time to embrace the impact of the possible devastation. Luckily, the cat surpassed our fall, and we took a deep breath. Surely, the dog came immediately after, crossing in our paths, and my cousin skillfully dodged ole Rufus."

Penelope continued, "Although, she wasn't as lucky a second go-around. Simone's bike and Rufus tangoed, rubber to flesh, as Rufus howled, and she went into mid-air, because the bike bounced her over her head, and landed on her pitiful knee cap." In their adolescence, she recalled the tender stages of their growth. They were much younger back then, leading up to junior high and high school memories."

Penelope waved at her friend at the counter checking out. "Ugh hmm. Did you leave anything behind for us to purchase in here?" she asked, as Chloe walked up with laughter to greet everyone.

"Well, knowing you, you're probably missing out on good deals because you're too busy doing more talking and less shopping. Hey, ladies! Guess who is with me? Tremaine is here. Now, it's really a mini reunion," Chloe said, excitedly.

Tremaine exited from the fitting room in a coral red, sleeveless romper, then looked in the direction of Chloe's voice to find out who she was talking to.

Penelope glanced over at Simone, trying to make eye contact. Then, Gigi naturally cleared her throat just to make sure Simone was okay. "Ahem." Simone nodded her head back, further away, in a calm gesture and temporarily avoided the reunion by browsing the hair products aisle instead. Penelope, Chloe, and Tremaine reached in for a group hug.

Penelope stared at Chloe then asked, "Do you remember Gigi's nickname when we were younger? The Bone Collector, because she was known for having the tea on everybody."

Chloe looked at Gigi, as she attempted to gather her thoughts, before replying, "She was The Bone Collector? Yea, I heard a lot about you. Hello, I'm Chloe. Nice to meet you. Gigi politely responded, "Likewise," as she's side-eyed Penelope with uncertainty.

"Sports was our lifeline during childhood. Track and field and basketball were two of the areas I pursued an interest," Chloe mentioned.

Tremaine stated, "I can attest that sports became a positive pastime in my life, too. We were all connected, very close during the track and field season. I truly believed these activities improved my overall health outcomes as an adult today, putting in core work back then."

Penelope said surprisingly, "I was so proud of how close we were then. I can recall nothing could come between us. The good days. Simone and I used to try and keep us all straight whenever we were mad at the other. Do you remember?"

Gigi decided to subliminally throw another bone by saying, "You do know Simone is here, right? Chloe have you seen her lately? She was standing over at the hair booth hoping to win a bundle of Malaysian hair with closures they are raffling."

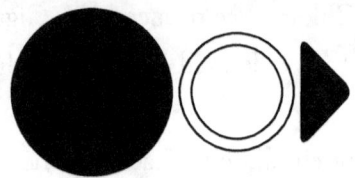

TREMAINE

Gigi led everyone in the direction where she last saw Simone. In the distance, they were approaching the refreshments for the attendees of the event. Immediately, Penelope picked up a few hors d'oeuvres of squash blossoms with pimento ricotta and crab toast as they walked by. Tremaine rolled her eyes and said, "That's Simone. The girl is fascinated with weave all day."

Gigi spotted Simone over where the refreshments were located, and then excused herself to grab some food of smoked shrimp, smoked salmon crisps, and toast spread bruschetta.

"Penny, I found her!" Gigi giggled with excitement. The only weird vibes Tremaine noticed consistently came from Simone, of course. There was an awkwardness between them. Without delay, Penny began to hug Simone and introduced her to Chloe.

Tremaine shared their history, "We had some good and bad days. We really have been through some hard-core tough times. Did you know it took me a very long time to get over when you stole Malcolm from me, Simone?"

Gigi went from sipping on her mimosa with class to gulping and chugging it back. "Oh, sugar honey iced tea."

"You intended to dig your dirty claws into my man for payback, Tre!?" Simone stopped drinking her ginger ale with a splash of cranberry juice. "Now, we are getting somewhere."

"Are we? I must admit I thoroughly enjoyed the satisfaction of seeing the look on your face that night." Tremaine said.

"Tremaine!" Penelope screamed in disgust.

"No, Penny, let her finish, so we all can know how trifling she can be. Cause that's two and a half decades of pain built up that she is just now addressing in her adult life," Simone said, while shaking her head in disbelief.

Tremaine asked, "Well, what could I say after Malcolm was murdered? Since, he was gone! What difference would it have made then anyhow?"

Epiphany: Selfish Traces of Tacky Footprints

The mere thought of how individuals can set out to become deceitful, injected with uncanny judgment of self-advances at the cost of others' abiding efforts. The fact that others will use resources, people, and talents for their own good is pure mischief. We are encouraged to consider *respectfulness, compassion, loyalty and forgiveness* in our daily lives. Although, there exists individuals that believe in putting their selfish desires above the law of camaraderie for a piece of tainted, temporary success.

As we continue to be fortunate to take breaths of air through our lungs, there are numerous encounters of family, friends, and co-workers' prejudged intentions to *intentionally* or *unintentionally* wreak havoc based on selfish decisions, daily. How does one proceed to pick up the raped, broken pieces of hard work after such disappointment? The true solution lies in attempting to have *compassion* throughout the entire process and *good stewardship*.

It is when we initially place compassion at the forefront of every new, existing, or old business or personal relationship. Each person should faithfully practice assessing every being in our network. We all are expected to fall short and drift off track during our lives. It has an effect due to our unique social and cultural background. Our personally kept assessments of individuals will provide enough evidence to determine a person's *liability rating*. Then, whenever faced with challenges of deceitfulness or attempts of conflict, we are not surprised, yet, prepared.

The ability to acknowledge closure is strength to stay focused during managing relationships. It is a *cleansing* experience to let go and *cut your losses*. Forgiveness is a must to ensure our efforts maintain on course. So, we can continue to grow our network *cautiously*. It is practicing these suggested solutions that will keep us all on track of our goals to success.

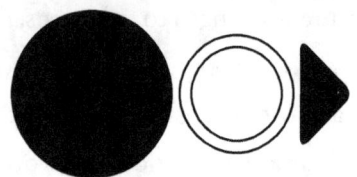

CHLOE

"Listen, we all have dealt with Malcolm's death differently. Because, some of us, whether we want to address it or not, haven't truly dealt with what happened. At least, I can admit openly that I am just now at a place in my life, at the age of thirty-four, where I can let it go and heal." Chloe grabbed her shopping bags, and everyone started leaving.

Tremaine agreed. "You're right, I observed how many times have you visited that Anaconda lady. Even though our mini-reunion was coincidental, it truly was great seeing everyone again. Malcolm would really be proud of our efforts today. I think he'd want all of us to stay strong and even grow closer to each other."

Admiring Simone's plumped belly, Penelope said, "I agree, Tremaine, we can get through our disagreements when we don't let anything or anyone come between us. This reunion was timely and orchestrated by God. I believe God is speaking to all of us at this very moment. He wants peace, healing, and forgiveness in our friendship. We all are beautifully made, melanin popping, sultry, sophisticated black queens. Let's make this a planned weekly or monthly gathering."

Simone started getting in the uber. "We mean too much to each other," she said. "Love you, ladies."

"Next meetup, Simone's baby shower!"

"Sounds great! Enjoyed you, ladies. See you later!"

Epiphany:
Artistic Influence!

The ability to genuinely express vivid examples of one thought and visions as it surpasses all human understanding. This type of illustration will leave grooves of vulnerabilities into your souls for the mere thought of challenging the controlled belief of historical traditions. These images tend to appear daring and dark with ill-will intentions lingering behind in the air for consumption.

As a child, we as humans can express our dreams and visions creatively in hopes of tapping into an array of artistic abilities. These expressions are valued as positive rays of energies to continue visualizing things into existence. The moment when our dreams and visions get larger, they become more tangible to reach. The momentum becomes contagious until your talents and gifts inspire others around you in your influential circle. Art will lead to the inner truth of self-expression to be genuinely imaginative, tapping into a clear consciousness of power. Discoveries of our distorted visions eventually translate to views in adulthood. Things begin to materialize right before us, into a pathway of common sense. We all possess the power to share knowledge to others. Self-empowerment is a gift of life.

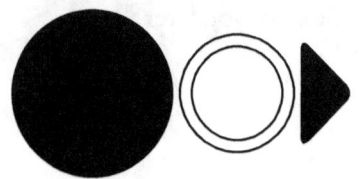

TREMAINE

Tremaine said, "I believe we truly care about each other's happiness. We may go about it the wrong way a lot of times. Although, I feel we have good intentions in the long haul. We need to forgive and love more. I pray and ask God to keep us and make us into the type of friends He wants us to be to each other."

Gigi agreed, "I'm just happy you ladies definitely don't look like all that you've been through."

Tremaine attested, "Well, I believe inhaling and smudging some quality sage did the trick!" The clique busted out with laughter.

"Smudging sage?" Gigi asked in disbelief.

"Hell yeah! Baby, don't sleep on sage. It will get rid of all that emotional crap going on with her, all while balancing her chakra. The smudging will concentrate on purging out the negative energy. It forces all the negative energy from your entire space, while restoring your mind," shouted Tremaine.

Chloe co-signed by covering her mouth to hide her huge smile. Tickled, she said, "I think I'm ready to try smudging. How do you go about it again?"

Tremaine giggled, "Now we are talking! See, first, you will need to get you one of those herb wands. Then, you really should concentrate on all corners, behind doors, and even smudge around the closets. But, when you are trying to cleanse an individual, all you should do is just fan the smoke all around yourself or the other person. Then, you must ask them to try and concentrate on pushing all the negative energy down through their toes. Most importantly, I highly recommend eating beets to heal your pussy."

Penelope raised her hand to signal the waiter. "Sir, I'm going to need another round of that Sun Kiss mimosa, please."

Gigi pointing her finger up in the air, as everyone began to laugh uncontrollably. "Make that three!" she said.

Chloe grabbed Tremaine's hand. "I apologize to you, Tremaine. I never knew you had feelings for Malcolm, because you had about ten other guys in rotation." They both burst into laughter.

Epiphany: Orchestrated Steps!

There are things in life, good or bad, already prepared for you so you can reach your destiny. The things we are given to embrace only can make you stronger. It is placed on a display for the world to witness your reactions. Then, there are times when we are undercover to most spectators, such as illness, loss of work, and death. These obstacles allow us to gain enough experience to possess the answers to help the next person in similar situations. It can help people to cope better, because of your obedience to share your story or testimony. A kind word or small act of kindness can brighten a person's day by lifting their hidden burdens. Whatever it may be, it will make a difference in the next person's struggle. Our assignments, obedience, passionate wisdom, and reflections will truly motivate and inspire others to move onward and not look back.

We sometimes ponder on the reasons why very chosen few are so willing to help the next person cope through their struggle. It is because we are instilled to be compassionate human beings. Our inner thoughts guide the directions to our actions. In our childhood, we are taught to be mindful, respectful to others, and do unto others as they do unto you.

Especially during the holiday season, there is always a helping hand in the time of need. We are very fortunate to experience favor. It should remind us that whatever we are doing, we are on the right track. It can be the monetary assistance you give to a nonprofit, or, it can be the occasional mentoring of little Calvin as he is roaming the neighborhood during his pastime, as you are heading to check the mailbox.

All of us are passionate about something in life, whether it is family, work, or school. This is what inspires you to take the next breath each day. It is the motivation behind your will to keep aiming to be successful. There is a great determination to utilize the wisdom attained from the many obstacles reflecting on the countless times we all have been unsuccessful.

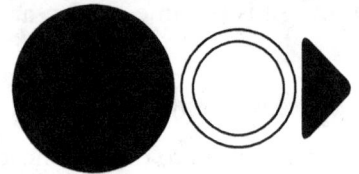

SIMONE

Surprisingly, when Simone arrived back at home, Charles was still there. There must have been a hurricane watch or something, because he's rarely home. Simone's shopping bags were filled with a few nice, inspirational wardrobe pieces to wear after dropping the excess baby weight.

"Hey, looks like you found some good deals at the pop up shop," Charles said, standing in the doorway of their bedroom. Is it a good time to finish our talk from earlier today? Here, let me take these from you." He reached down to grab the shopping bags to carry over to the dresser countertop inside the bedroom.

"Thank you. Yes we can talk." Chuck drew near to reach for Simone's hand while she sat on the California king size bed.

"Baby, I know I messed up and you may be considering leaving me," he said. "Baby don't leave. I will make this right. Those women were just an illusion. You are my reality. I love you."

Simone sat there listening, then she moved her head. "One of those women you decided to have an affair with is my close childhood friend. She was allowed into our home. Yet, to your surprise, all of this betrayal was a setup to bless me to continue. God surely knew what He was doing when He made me. Rest assured that He prepares a table in front of me in the presence of my enemies, all day every day. I'm a lot wiser now. For starters, I know now that I must stop running towards the folks who ignore me. Instead, I will start running towards those who attentively adore me," she said, confidently.

"Actually, is it ok...can you please pray for me first?"

Oh, he knew how Simone felt about the power of prayer. So, mutually, she agreed the Lord is the only one who could revive them at this moment. Simone held his hand and begin to cry out, "Lord, Charles and I come to you asking for your forgiveness and mercy. Lord, I pray that you create a clean heart in Charles; reintroduce an unwavering soul inside. I'm pleading, don't cast him out from your presence, Lord. Please don't remove your holy spirit from his reach. God, I come, asking you to prevent him from complaining, cursing, and grumbling. Lord, teach Charles to be a better husband and a good father. Lord, please remove anyone or anything from his life that would provoke temptation to infidelity. We ask for you to bring unity between Charles and I on this day. Lord, teach me what to say and how to say it on behalf of my husband. I ask that you make us whole again, into a cohesive team and no separation. We ask these things in Jesus' name. Amen."

Charles' phone sounded continuously from an unsaved number. He wondered who it was then answered. "Hello," he asked, then paused as he listened carefully to the other caller on the line.

"Listen very closely, you may feel like you dodged a silver bullet regarding your white picket fence, and glasshouse situation, but, I want you to know one thing..."

Charles immediately recognized the caller's tone, it was Tremaine. Yet, Charles maintained his composure to prevent more conflict in his failing marriage as he replied, "What is it?"

Tremaine continued, "I am not the one you want to try and run-over. I will expect you to treat me the same as before. Is that a problem?"

Chuck appeared dazed, with his head tilted towards the floor. "I got it," he replied, as he clinched on to the phone tightly.

"I am expecting your child, and yes, I am planning on keeping it. So, I want you to understand, anything contrary to that understanding is your problem. Are we clear?"

"We clear," he said, as he was left holding on to the phone long enough to hear the dial tone in the background.

Epiphany: Your Outlook on Life Can Cost You Your Life!

Words are merely figurative meanings of what your inner being speaks internally. Yet, the actions placed forth, with the choice of words, yields spiritual dividends. When these dividends are valuable is extremely up to the captured audience. Hopefully, through a living testament, spirits are set free and yokes are broken. When I was given an opportunity to express my inner thoughts in a public platform such as this one, I doubted myself. I thought to myself, *"No one will get it due to their critical judgments of approval."* Yet, I kept reflecting on the potential outlook it could have on lives. Hopefully, this will resonate until a blessing of favor erodes!

By pushing forward, we can overthrow self-doubt. I truly wonder how much further this planet we live in could be, at this very moment, if we can set aside the utility bill, daycare expense, or rapid project deadlines. Then, we can reflect on our beautiful capital city's growth. In fact, we can contribute and make it a safer environment for our youth. It could potentially eliminate a few of the gang related, homicide, or child abuse statistics. Perhaps, it would multiply more family togetherness or wholesome workplace team building activities.

In conclusion, only during sporadic broken routine activities, will you be allowed to notice strong, routine activity exists. During the hustle and bustle of necessary routines, we should allow adjustments that spark spontaneity for positive change. Our daily routines, like examples referred to above, can cause the time to slip by; until, you lose opportunities on the precious things that matters. Time waits on no one. It is these things which can inadvertently cost you your life.

What does a champion look like? They are approachable, caring, loving, trustworthy, respected, transparent, inspiring, resilient, enthusiastic, praised, and recognized.

Unless you are suspecting someone is involved in trafficking, get help. For instance, observing your loved one's routine. Are they free to come and go as they wish? Involved in underage commercial sex acts on top of that, are they getting paid or receiving monetary tips for their abnormal activities? Some children are conditioned to their environment to assume it to be normal conditions.

Have you noticed any high security measures around their living situation, such as cameras, barbed wire fencing, boarded up windows, or something unusual, you know? Even the potential victim behavior is different, like they won't look you directly in the eyes. Or, he or she is not in control of their own financial affairs, or looks malnourished. If you answered yes, then you should seek help immediately.

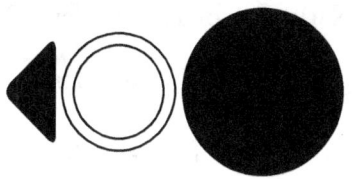

RESOURCES

U.S. Equal Employment Opportunity Commission 800-669-4000

U.S. Department of Health Human Services Food & Drug Administration 888-463-6332

Physicians Committee for Responsible Medicine 202-686-2210

National Human Genome Research Institute 301-402-0911

National Suicide Prevention Lifeline toll-free at 800-273-8255

Substance Abuse & Mental Health Services Administration National Helpline 800-662-4357

Suicide Awareness Voices of Education (SAVE) www.save.org

Mental Health Hotline 877-726-4727

National Alliance on Mental Illness 800-950-6264

National Human Trafficking Hotline 888-373-7888

Thorn, Inc. Anti-Child Sex Trafficking info@wearethorn.org

Think of Us, Inc. Foster Care info@thinkof-us.org

National Child Abuse Hotline 800-422-4453

National Domestic Violence Hotline: 800-799-7233

Boys Town 800-448-3000

Crisis Text Line Text HOME to 741741

National Hopeline Network 800-442-4673

PTSD Foundation of America Veteran Line: 877-717-7873

Lifeline for Vets 888-777-4443

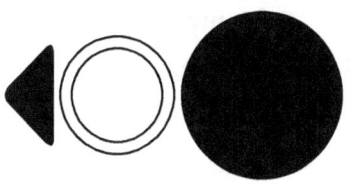

ABOUT THE AUTHOR

Sherika is the daughter of Mr. Walter Frazier and Emma Cherry Frazier of Madison, Florida. She is a proud mother of two beautiful children: a sixteen-year-old daughter, Nia Janae Duncan and twelve-year-old son, Nyles J'Sean Duncan. She is a Tallahassee native, originally from Madison, Florida. A devoted sister to one brother, Mr. Walter Frazier, Jr. of Stone Mountain, Georgia. A loving sister-in-law to Pamela Barnes Frazier, and aunt to two nephews, Walter Brandon Frazier and Bradley Eugene Frazier of Stone Mountain, Georgia. She is a loving niece to a host of uncles and aunts. (Dorothy Frazier Joseph (deceased), Dr. John Frazier, Ola Frazier Hart, Clara Frazier Patterson, Rosa Frazier Aikens, Windford Frazier, Effie Frazier Owens, Darren Williams, John Williams, Bobby Cherry, Rosa Mary Cherry, (Henry Cherry (deceased), (Jerome Cherry (deceased), Albert and Andrew Cherry (twins), Horace Cherry, Cynthia Cherry Akins, Angela Cherry; and a very special cousin to Mary Ghee, Kimberly Alexander, Cornelius Cherry, Felicia Cherry McDaniel, Sheila Joseph Reddick, Jasmin Richardson, Malinda Cherry Williams and Collette Cherry Glee). She is the Executive Director of a 501c3 nonprofit performing art organization, Excellence Dance Studio, Inc. She holds an MBA degree with a specialization in project management from the Forbes School of Business at

Ashford University. She is a past SEMCoP Science Engineering Math & Computers scholar who obtained a Bachelor of Science in Computer Information Systems and business minor from Florida Agricultural & Mechanical University on a full honors scholarship, in addition to, the assistance of a Minority Community College Transfer Scholarship. She earned an Associate of Arts degree from North Florida Community College. Freelance Blogger for Tallahassee.com Community sections. Recently she is a graduate of the prestigious Florida State University Reubin O'D Askew School of Public Administration and Policy Florida Center for Public Management Certified Public Manager Leadership Program and formerly affiliated in National Association of University Women, International & F.&A.M. Order of Eastern Star, Madison County Chapter of the Charmettes, Inc., Toastmaster International Profound Sound for Public Speaking. Excellence Dance Studio, Inc. is a federally recognized tax-exempt organization under section 501(c)(3) servicing the community at large, for more info contact (850) 270-1226. for more info about Sherika visit www.sherikaduncan.com

Connect with Sherika Duncan

To schedule a booking with Sherika Duncan for your upcoming event, seminar or consultation needs visit:

Website: www.sherikaduncan.com
Facebook: SherikaDuncanAuthor
Instagram: sherika.duncan
Twitter: SherikaDuncan_
YouTube: Sherika Duncan
Email: sherika@sherikaduncan.com

www.ingramcontent.com/pod-product-compliance
Lightning Source LLC
Chambersburg PA
CBHW071237080526
44587CB00013BA/1648